The Safety Godmothers

The ABCs of Awareness, Boundaries and Confidence for Teens

Ellen Snortland

and

Lisa Gaeta

•

Edited by Ken Gruberman

D1469141

B3 Books

ALTADENA

The Safety Godmothers
The ABCs of Awareness, Boundaries and Confidence for Teens

Authors: Ellen Snortland and Lisa Gaeta
Editor: Ken Gruberman
Cover and Publication Design: Marty Safir, Double M Graphics

Published by
B3 Books
Altadena, California

ISBN 978-0-9711447-3-6

9 8 7 6 5 4 3 2 1

"The Safety Godmothers" is dedicated
to the Gaetas, the Snortlands and all the
families who love and encourage passion,
leadership and boldness in their daughters.

Contents

Appendix

For Parents Only

By Gavin de Becker, bestselling author of *The Gift of Fear* and *Protecting the Gift*

Among all the possible risks we might face — from the freak accident to the predictable accident, from the chemical under the sink to the chemical sold on the street corner — nothing is more frightening to us than the danger posed by people, the danger that is by design, the danger that is conscious.

The danger that is conscious may reside within the neighborhood teenage boy who makes us uncomfortable, or the babysitter we do not trust, or the mall security guard who stares at our daughter, or the deliveryman who gives her an unsolicited gift. Though many people act as if it's invisible, the danger that is conscious is usually in plain view; disguised perhaps, but in plain view nonetheless. Some of the behaviors that precede this kind of danger are designed to distract, confuse, or reassure us, but those behaviors are themselves signals. There is a universal code of violence, and you already know that code.

Think of a newborn baby girl. She is the latest model of human being, the proud result of millenia of R&D that makes the most fantastic computer seem like an abacus. She has more brain cells than you and me combined, more in fact, than there are grains of sand on your favorite beach. She can learn, teach, design, build. She has within her the cleverness and dexterity to catch an ant or a whale. She can fly — literally. She can travel to another planet, and many of her contemporaries will.

Can you believe, even for a moment, that this astonishing being was designed without a defense system? Nature's investment in this child is far too great for such an oversight. For the earliest years in a child's life, parents are the defense system designed to spot danger at the earliest possible moment, and qualified to avoid it, evade it, escape it, or destroy it.

As the years go on, whose responsibility that is becomes less clear. Does it still belong to the parents, or is it now with the daycare center, or the parents of your child's friend, or the school, or the mall, or the police, or the university, or the government? And a question particularly significant for readers of this book: when does a daughter *herself* take over? Is it the first time she is allowed to be alone in the house or the first time she walks herself to school? Or is it that afternoon when she first backs the car down the driveway (and over the sidewalk) into the street?

While a woman might get far in life without having to acknowledge that violence is a part of humanity, once she becomes a mother, she will have to powerfully come to terms with it. Violence, though rarely humane, is always human. It is around our children, and it is both in them and us — meaning it can also be a resource when needed. Ellen Snortland and Lisa Gaeta help to make this resource available in these pages, and through their other teaching and programs. When I discuss this point in speeches, there is usually someone, often a timid woman, who raises her hand

and says, "I could never be violent; I could never hurt another person." But if I just wait, she will add a telling caveat: "… unless, of course, someone tried to harm my child." In that event, this timid woman not only might hurt a person, she would want to. She who said she could never be violent would now hit, punch, scratch, bite, rip, shoot, stab — so the violence *is* in her, ready to emerge like an assassin if need be. Nature is ruthless, and rather than seek to deny mankind's cruelties, we can accept and draw upon the resources within us — even the ones we wish weren't necessary.

You may have gotten this far in life without the confidence that you can protect yourself, but you'll benefit from accepting that you are a creature of nature, fully endowed with powerful defenses.

You can become unwilling to relinquish your control to a predator, and you can — after all these years — stop caring about politeness! As parent and child advocate Anna McDonnell says, "To have a child is to have the chance to revisit your own childhood and self, and sometimes to make changes that have been needed for a long while."

Sad to say, but important to know: Teenage girls are the most victimized segment of our population and, at the same time, the least likely to report a crime. Why? For starters, they offer less resistance and they pose less risk than adult women. Next, teenage girls are perceived as sexual objects, prohibited perhaps, but sexual nonetheless. The issue is complicated by the fact that teenage girls are themselves exploring the dynamics of male attention and they want to be accepted by men. Some girls mix the youthful feeling of immortality with budding sexuality, seeing fearlessness as a form of sophistication. This coincides with enhanced vulnerability and exposure, since teenage girls are now at the age where they can be away from parental supervision, to take a first job, have a first date, experiment with drugs and alcohol.

Surprisingly, for many women who rescue themselves from a violent encounter through cleverness or use of force, the experience of victimization can actually be favorable. Prevailing over a predator can leave a woman empowered, more confident, and more competent to meet the challenges of life. I know women who suffered greatly after experiencing a crime of domination or force, and I know others who flourished. The key difference lies in the victim's perception of how she managed the situation.

What victims often need to find or recover is the belief that they are competent to protect themselves. And here we come to one of the big gifts Ellen and Lisa offer: the awareness that you are *designed* to protect yourself, and competent to do so.

We all must learn and re-learn that, if you cannot change the environment, you can almost always change the situation. And this book offers some of the best teaching on how to do that. Thank you, Ellen. Thank you, Lisa — for the gift you are giving in these pages, and for letting me be part of your important IMPACT work over the years.

Gavin de Becker

February, 2014

Introduction

THE ABCs OF PERSONAL SAFETY

Welcome to our world! We are Lisa Gaeta and Ellen Snortland — **The Safety Godmothers** — of IMPACT Personal Safety of Southern California. We teach people of all ages how to respond to an immediate threat from a violent person by training them as realistically as possible. We don't think talking about "what if" is enough, which is why we stage verbal and physical mock attacks in the safest way we can. This involves having our students learn to verbally set boundaries and then, if the talking is not enough, to physically defend themselves.

This type of realistic "adrenaline-state" training is similar to the training received by first responders, such as law enforcement, fire fighters and paramedics. We firmly believe that *everyone* needs to know how to be their own first responder, because no matter how much law enforcement personnel want to stop the bad guys, they can never respond as quickly as you can in the seconds that make the most difference during an assault. Besides IMPACT, we also endorse other empowerment based self-defense courses; see our referrals at the end of the book.

We are committed to your safety and happiness, in the same

way the Fairy Godmothers were concerned about Sleeping Beauty in the famous fairytale. If you go back and watch the classic Disney animated version of "Sleeping Beauty," notice that the real heroes of the story are the ditzy, fluttery and generous Fairy Godmothers. They got in the way of Maleficent's evil plan and made sure her spell on Aurora would fail to kill the princess when she pricked her finger on the spinning wheel later in her life. It would have been an entirely different story without the intervention from those 3 determined visitors, along with their christening wishes of intelligence, grace and beauty.

Our mission is also to intervene: we are here to let you know that you are designed by Mother Nature herself to be self-protective. We are here to bestow you with blessings just as important as the ones from the Fairy Godmothers: the safety blessings of awareness, boundaries and confidence. And — if push comes to actual shove — the blessing of some serious ass-kicking skills.

Mother Nature

Mother Nature gave us lots of tools to protect ourselves. You know that flinch response that has you automatically protect your face when something flies toward you? If it's a ball, most of us will catch it. If it's something else, our hands move quickly and automatically to keep our eyes safe. Thanks Mother Nature! By the same token, when it comes to protecting ourselves in a physical confrontation, we know that a predator needs to see and we use the assailant's flinch response against him. We go for the eyes, and when he instinctively protects them we target something else!

Mother Nature also gave us chemicals that help us to stay safe. We'll talk more about this later in the book. For now, know that adrenaline is a very strong chemical. It's designed to save your life, but if you're not used to it, adrenaline can be maddening or paralyzing. You would not want to put your trust in the hands of a paramedic, peace officer or emergency room doctor who is unable to manage their adrenaline. That is why emergency service providers train under as realistic conditions as possible. That is also the idea behind the way we train: our simulated attacks are as close to "real" as we can get, so our students can learn to function with adrenaline and not hurt themselves or others while they practice. We think that teens should have an adrenaline-based course like ours before getting their drivers' licenses, since managing adrenaline is also an important part of driving a car, which is a dangerous piece of machinery.

Our padded assailant instructors (they can be male or female, depending on the location) dress in protective, padded suits that allow them to take full force, full impact hits for hours at a time. Our students actually experience what it takes to physically engage with assailants while defending themselves… and yes, also managing their very real adrenaline surges effectively.

Why Did We Write This Book?

While the wisdom we strive to impart in this book applies to everyone, we will be focusing on girls and women most of the time. Why is that? For decades, the media in all forms (now including the Internet) has been chock-full of images and stories about girls and women that typically involve attacks, rapes, and victimization. This non-stop deluge reinforces the notion that women and girls are both helpless and powerless to defend themselves. Scant coverage is given to the brave people (including females) who successfully defend themselves without a weapon, which helps to keep these bogus ideas in place. There are many success stories that aren't included in the national conversation about violence prevention. We want to shift the conversation from "everyone knows it's impossible" for a girl or woman to defend herself, to "it's *definitely* possible!" with our many examples of "Oh yes she did!" that you'll find in this book.

We've selected our favorite success stories from the hundreds given to us by our students over the years. We also share a few success stories from people who have not studied with us, as they illustrate important lessons. In *every* story, regardless of the source, we've changed identifying factors to respect privacy, but we assure you the main points of each story really happened.

We've organized this book so it can be read either cover to cover, or in any order you choose simply by picking a letter of the alphabet. And we have a special guest: Gavin de Becker, a Safety Godfather if you will, who shares his wisdom in two sections and provides a special message to parents.

Each alphabetical letter starts with a success story or student testimonial, which is followed by our often irreverent "How We See It" commentary. This is where we give you our blow-by-blow analysis of the success story: what worked, what didn't work, and what you might learn from the specific incident. We then delve into a topic that is related to the story. For instance, "A is for AWARENESS" and so on, through the entire alphabet.

In addition, we have included some of our favorite survey answers from our students. At IMPACT we often survey our students to find out how their lives have changed both before, during and after taking our training, and some of the answers we receive are priceless! In a way, you'll be making the same kind of journey while reading this book, and we've included a similar survey just for you. You'll find the collection of our favorite survey responses, along with your own survey, at the very end of the book so you can see for yourself how your perceptions change as you progress through the chapters.

Another item you'll find at the back of the book is a special "References" section. We specifically designed this book to be both serious and fun, as the topic of self-defense — especially for girls and women — can make some people squirm just thinking about it. We often defuse that "squirm" factor with humor, because that's just who we are! At the same time, we are delving into some serious issues that affect all of us, and we don't want to downplay that. Throughout the book we make some pretty audacious statements, based on numerous studies, statistics and citations. Rather than bore you with the details, we've put them all (and more) in the References section so you can quickly access the facts and figures if you are interested.

If you notice some overlap, that's OK. Educators and students know repetition is an important part of learning, whether with physical or intellectual education. Since most of our readers will be relatively new to the entire notion of self-defense, especially for girls and women, we think it's important to reinforce key ideas.

While most of our heroes are young women, we've also included a few adult women, a couple of men, and a boy to the mix. Why? Because we can all learn from each other regardless of our age or gender. After reading this book, you'll know more about personal safety than a huge portion of the population, certainly more than most of your elders!

One of the most important things we can do is encourage your imagination. We want you to say, "If she or he can do that, *I* can do that!" Yes, you can. If you can imagine it, you can do it yourself. We are also honored to witness, and now share, how courageous our students are. While it's true that fear can be contagious, we know from experience that courage is also contagious and can be passed forward.

We offer these explorations and success stories as antidotes to the non-stop flood of reports in the media that tend to scare the living daylights out of most of us. We've written this book for you and your friends, to let you know about amazing, funny and inspiring stories that have been kept from you: stories about other teens, women, older people, and even kids, all proving that bravery and wits can be used to outwit what are usually cowardly and often numbskull bullies and predators.

We think of what we do as vital to a well-rounded, basic education, so we're serious about it. However, that doesn't mean that we're somber — we *love* to have fun!

Similarly, we see how much fun our students have with the type of full force, full impact self-defense we teach at IMPACT Personal Safety and our sister chapters and allies all over the world. There are those of us who are truly excited by the adrenaline rush we experience when a padded mock assailant grabs us from behind. It's exciting to quickly gather our wits and skills and then beat the "pretend" attacker back, and then into a "knockout." That's the sports and athletic part of what we do, and it's a blast for many of us!

We invite you to see yourselves in these stories. They are about people just like you. After all, you are part of the human family and as such, we believe you have the right to defend yourself. But first, you must be taught! And while reading a book is not the same as doing, our brains learn a lot from stories.

Shameless Self-Promotion

Of *course* we want you to attend our classes! We've spent decades refining our courses and techniques, and we know they work. Why then are we sharing our decades' worth of collective experience with you? Because we know it's not always possible for you to take a class from us, or anyone else. Is reading a book the same as attending a class? Again, no. However, learning can still be achieved by reading, and even one sentence that resonates with you can open up new horizons. We know of one young woman who saved herself from a violent predator because she'd heard on the radio that if you kick an assailant's knee, it'll break. That's what she did and it worked, even though she'd never physically practiced kicking out someone else's knee.

No matter what class you take, or if you take a class at all, we want you to know up-front that this is not a teaching book. We're not going to provide you with step-by-step lessons. Instead, we are going to give you inspiration through eye-opening real stories of courage and bravery you've never heard before. The brain is so powerful that we know you'll get valuable information just from reading about a success that happened with someone else.

Women and Men

A word about men vs. women. We are not anti-male; we are *anti-violence*. Most of the time we train with a female and male co-instructor team, which sends a strong message: it is through *partnership* with men and women that we'll finally end violence. We feel strongly about female and male partnership in taking on the epidemic of violence against women and girls. Yes, boys and men are attacked too, but the difference is they do not have to struggle with the cultural "norm" women and girls inherit: that they are defenseless by virtue of their gender. While we also train men and boys, our primary focus is on women and girls.

In this book, we use "he" and "him" almost exclusively in discussions about violence because the vast majority of the time, the perpetrator of violence against a female is male. Yes, there are violent females, but they are the exception, not the rule. Sadly, there are a great many kind, gentle men who are feared simply by virtue of their gender, but it's very difficult at first glance to tell a non-violent man from a violent one, since "I'm a predator" is rarely tattooed on the foreheads of rapists or assailants.

Credibility

Why should you listen to us? Because we've taught *thousands* of people over the course of thousands of hours. We've been on television for decades reaching millions of viewers, including shows like Oprah, Dateline NBC, 48 Hours and even sitcoms. You should check out the great parody of our class on the 6th season premiere of *King of the Hill* called "Bobby Goes Nuts." (You can find clips of it on YouTube.) There's hardly anything we haven't encountered when it comes to students. We've taught people with cerebral palsy, folks who can't see or hear, who use wheelchairs or have debilitating physical conditions, and people suffering with post-traumatic stress from violent incidents in their past. We've taught thousands of women, hundreds of men and thousands of high school age girls in Southern California, where many of our success stories take place. The location doesn't matter, though; our students could use what they've learned anywhere in the world, and you can too.

So… prepare to read a book that will alter the way you look at violence and personal safety in news stories, movies, TV, and most importantly, your life. We want you to walk away saying, "Thank you, Safety Godmothers. My safety is vital and I *am* my own first responder." You're welcome.

Common Objections, Concerns and Misconceptions

A common reaction, when prospective students consider signing up for a class, is "It's not *fair*! Why should *we* have to learn how to defend ourselves? The violent ones should stop being violent!" We totally agree that violent men and boys should stop being violent. However, the males that are interested in being violent are not listening to us… so far. It might take a good knee to the groin to make some of them hear what we're saying, which is "Stop!"

Students often ask "what if making a scene or fighting back makes him mad?" The thought behind it being, "I'm afraid I might make him mad and therefore, make the situation worse." **The Safety Godmothers** become frustrated sometimes, because this kind of thinking blames the victim — you! It's not your fault in any way that you are being attacked; it's not because you made it worse by making him mad. You cannot turn a normal man into an assailant by making him mad… you simply can't.

When students ask this question, "What if I make him mad?" we often answer with, "What if he makes *you* mad?" We're serious! Why is it okay to spare his feelings, the guy who is poised to hurt you? He doesn't give a hoot about you, so why are you worried about him? And remember, he's just a big ego-scarred scaredy-cat anyway, and you can certainly outwit him.

Another classic we hear: "Aren't your students too young to confront violence?" We think not. According to Love Is Respect.com, (http://www.loveisrespect.org) "Violent behavior typically begins between the ages of 12 and 18." Dating violence is very real. Boys who control their girlfriends are just as dangerous as adult men who thrash the women and kids in their lives.

If a boy you like shoves or hits, stop seeing him and get help immediately. Sadly, we don't have super accurate statistics about intimate violence between minors because a lot of girls don't want to get their boyfriends in trouble or get in trouble themselves. A girl who has just won the freedom to date is often reluctant to report something that will result in *her* losing her independence; handling intimate violence is complicated, and oftentimes just as complicated in teens' lives as adult lives.

As far as how young a person can be to learn personal safety skills? **The Safety Godmothers** truly believe that kids should learn personal safety skills at the same time they begin learning traffic safety skills. Some people say, "Oh man, wouldn't that scare the child?" Not really. Kids don't walk around being afraid of cars, even though they know that cars are potentially dangerous. And they actually feel better when things are explained to them. So, too, should kids learn how to deal with people who are bothering them; that "bothering" can be as mild as teasing, all the way up to actual molestation or kidnapping.

Kid personal safety skills are easy to learn, and they stay with the student forever. As the student gets older, more mature content is added that addresses such things as dating, and how to deal with inappropriate or violent behavior from people they know.

We have heard parents tell us they are concerned that their daughters will become "unlady-like" if they learn how to fight back. If we had a nickel for every time someone told us it was *unlady-like* to raise our voices or to defend ourselves, we'd be some filthy rich Safety Godmothers!

Seriously, imagine an animal who is unable to defend itself. Absurd. Not "natural." Nature does not create beings that cannot defend themselves! Even *plants* defend themselves, and if you don't agree, go argue with poison oak or grab a rose bush without gloves.

No one who is about to be attacked by a rabid dog checks its gender first, and then says, "oh, it's just a girl dog…" and turns their back. Ladylike? Puh-leaze! If your life is in danger, there is likely going to be no one else around who is available and capable to defend you; it'll be just you, and *only* you. Consider this: some people say, "It's not lady-like to defend yourself!" We say, "Oh, but it *is* lady-like to be beaten up or killed?" Right.

Finally, **the Safety Godmothers** are keen on good manners and etiquette. We teach "anti-etiquette" for those who ignore THEIR good manners. People pleasing and good manners are two completely different things.

How many of us have forced ourselves to stay seated in a movie theater or sporting event when some weirdo sits right next to us, even though there are plenty of empty seats nearby? Our NOT switching seats is based on the "good manners" most of us were brought up with. However, our guardians did not tell us what to do when the hackles go up on the back of our neck, and yet we don't want to hurt this complete stranger's feelings... *Really?* What is stopping us from simply getting up and changing seats?

What about the sleazy guy who persists in asking us out, or buying us dinner, or getting us a coffee and we let him, so as to not upset *him*? This is "people pleasing" at its most damaging. You are basically selling out the importance of your own time to the desires of this person you don't want to be with. And it's not just with members of the opposite sex.

What about that annoying friend who is consistently late: you hate her chronic lateness, but won't say anything because you don't want to seem petty or too demanding? Again, you're basically letting her time be more important than yours, by letting it go without a talk about what would work better for you. Why would you do that? We suggest it's because you don't want to displease whomever it is that you're not telling the truth to... the date you never wanted to be on, or the friend whose habits drive you crazy.

OK, so all of this people pleasing stuff is *very* normal, and you shouldn't let the fact that you have people pleased before make you feel badly about yourself now. What we want is for you to examine behaviors that go against your instincts. That's where people pleasing can cost you more than time... it can cost you self-respect, and worse, it can cost you your safety.

Two Common Terms Used in This Book

1 "No!"

That is the first and most basic "term" we teach and pass on; how to say "No" and mean it. And how to back up your "No" with physical self-defense if and when it's needed.

2 Ready Stance

We refer to ready stance in various stories. **The Safety Godmothers** think it's a good idea to get into ready stance whenever you need to deal with situations that range from standing up for yourself, to actually fighting for your life. Ready stance goes like this:

Both feet flat on the ground, hip-width apart, right leg back, knees slightly bent. Hands up and elbows in; if it is a low-level situation, your hands will be up about shoulder level and should be relaxed as if your hands were saying, "calm down." If it is a dangerous situation, your hands are up in front of your face to protect yourself from swings and punches.

We also use what is effectively a ready stance if you're on the ground: that is, hands in front of the face, and legs between you and the assailant.

We believe that the rest of the skills we teach and describe in the following stories are self-explanatory.

The Safety Godmothers

ABBY ATTACKS BACK

Abby was walking home from a friend's house one evening in a "nice neighborhood" of Los Angeles, one she was very familiar with. Although it was dark, she felt comfortable there, even walking in the alley as she'd done for years. Abby was 15. Suddenly, she was violently grabbed from behind.

The first thing she did was bite the man's arm and he let go of her. The next thing Abby knew, the assailant was on the ground and neighbors were coming to see what the commotion was about.

Abby's assailant was injured so severely he needed an ambulance. His knee was broken, as was his nose, and his testicles were severely bruised and swollen.

Abby does not remember all the details; she only knows that when he grabbed her, she yelled "NO!"

and soon after remembers hearing him yell, "Stop, you're hurting me!" Ohhhh, poor baby.

As it turns out, the assailant was a wanted rapist; authorities had been searching for him in connection with several rapes of young girls in the area. He was taken into custody when the paramedics put him into the ambulance and called the police.

HOW WE SEE IT

Although we aren't sure how anyone actually found out that the guy — who definitely puts the "ass" in assailant — had swollen and bruised testicles (ewwww!), we're sure it's true. Why? Because Abby had been trained on how to break a knee, and also how to send *her* knee crashing into a groin… not dissimilar to the upward swing of a wrecking ball, or in this case, wrecking *balls*.

Abby is proof that adrenaline-based training kicks in without any intellectual engagement. She had trained her body to react, and react it did. In this instance, not only did Abby not have to think about how to protect herself, she can't even remember doing it!

This reminds us of the occasional news story about mothers who perform heroic deeds when someone they love is in grave danger, or strangers who do amazing things when someone is in peril. Adrenaline can be considered a miracle chemical which can transform regular people into Super Heroes. And in Abby's case, adrenaline gave her power, as well as erasing her short-term memory.

One of our goals at IMPACT Personal Safety is to train women and girls to be as passionate about protecting themselves as they are about protecting children or others.

Abby will be a great Mom, if that's the path she takes, by being an example for her daughters and/or sons that a woman is just as able to protect herself as a man. She kneed the assailant in both senses of the term: kneed him in the groin, and *kneed* him — as in brought him down by breaking his knee. Very few people know how vulnerable a knee is. It takes only 15 pounds of force to break one and virtually anyone can do it if they know how. If you can kick out a knee, we guarantee your erstwhile assailant will be "kneeding" an ambulance!

A is for AWARENESS

Many of our senses are early warning systems: we hear a noise that alerts us, we smell odors that tell us there's a gas leak or a fire. Our peripheral vision is more than a vehicle driving aid — it notices objects and movement from outside our direct vision wherever we are. We have innate reflexes, flinch responses, fight-or-flight reactions, all designed to keep us safe. These are all parts of being aware and alive.

Awareness of our surroundings is part of our defense system. Likewise, bodies are designed to protect themselves. *All* animal species — and even some plant species — have automatic responses to danger that keep themselves and their offspring safe. Human beings are the only species that will frequently second guess their natural instincts.

In the preceding story, *Abby Attacks Back*, awareness doesn't seem to be in play, at least in her conscious awareness. She was in an alley that she was familiar with, so perhaps her guard was down a bit, compared to being in a strange alley. Nonetheless, her animal awareness kicked in — so to speak — when she fought with all her might when she was ambushed, just like any other mammal. Her senses didn't pick up her assailant but her body certainly reacted when he grabbed her.

For example, if a deer senses something that could be a predator, it doesn't ignore it by telling itself, "It's nothing! You're just being silly…" It freezes, hoping to blend into the scenery, then flees as quickly as it can. It does not say, "Oh, gosh, I don't want to hurt that predator's feelings so I'll pretend I'm not creeped out." But we humans do just that.

Intentional awareness skills can be learned, and help us gather information for our natural response system to process. These learned awareness skills can become habits, like looking both ways before you cross the street; if you forget, you might get hit by a car. For most of us, looking both ways is now so ingrained that we never forget to do it … but it wasn't always that way. Someone had to teach us. In that vein, we encourage safety practices similar to other forms of prevention.

To prime the "awareness pump" during our IMPACT kids' classes, we play games and give assignments to our students, such as "What's new in my neighborhood?" We ask our students to come back to the next class with a verbal report. We suggest, as they leave their residences every morning, they do a visual check around their houses or apartments:

- Are the screens intact?
- Are bushes trampled?
- Are the neighbors home?
- Are there any open windows or doors?
- Any unfamiliar cars, utility trucks, cable trucks, moving vans, etc.

We encourage them to look for things that might be out of the ordinary by first recognizing what's ordinary. In truth, these practices can benefit people of all ages.

When you know what is "normal" while at home, work, school or elsewhere, then our bodies and intuition will alert us when things are off, odd or creepy. This allows us to be alert and pay more attention if and when it's necessary.

We once had a student in an adult class who, during an orientation circle, answered the question "Why are you here?" by saying that she hadn't slept since her son was born. The other women in the circle who were mothers nodded supportively with the knowledge of how exhausting a newborn can be. She said that every noise woke her up. More nods of sympathy. We told her that post-partum insomnia was normal and after a while she would relax and be able to sleep through the night.

When she then told us her son was *10 years old*, we saw it was necessary to have her do some homework. Her assignment was to lay in bed every night before falling asleep and just listen to her house; it would make the same noises each night as it cooled down, the electric appliances would whirr on and off at regular intervals, and she would soon learn the unique rhythm and feel of her own surroundings.

The next week she came back to class and said she did her homework for three nights in a row and had slept through the night every night since! IMPACT success stories are often like this: they don't necessarily involve a confrontation with another person. This student had to confront the fear she had for 10 years in her own home, in her own bed. Once she knew what was normal, she would only be awakened by a sound, smell or feeling that didn't fit.

It's helpful to do awareness exercises for other parts of your life as well. We tend to drop our defenses when we are in familiar places, such as our schools, the workplace and recreational areas. Therefore familiar places are most commonly where we will be targeted by people who are on the lookout for those who are unaware. On the other hand, someone who is constantly concerned and worried about their surroundings suffers from what is called hyper-vigilance, and it's exhausting and non-productive to live that way. You can train your awareness and trust your intuition (See *I is for Intuition*) to do the job for you rather than being hyper-vigilant.

Projecting confidence (even if you don't feel that way),

looking like someone who knows where they are going, and being someone who is willing to look around and monitor their environment gives you many advantages for well-being.

We coach people to monitor others when they are out and about, but not in an intense way. We tell them to let people know *you* know they are there by making eye contact, instead of avoiding it as most people do in the guise of "politeness." By the same token, don't stare people down: if you are uncomfortable with eye contact, look at some part of their body like the shoulders or chin. We know that in some cultures it's completely taboo for a woman to look a man straight in the eyes, which is another reason why looking at an alternate area might be a good idea. The point is simply to *look* and be aware.

Too many women and girls have the attitude, "Oh no, here comes a creepy guy. I don't want to hurt his feelings. Maybe if I don't look at him he'll just go away. If I don't see him he won't be there." Of course we know this is not the case. Paradoxically, doing just the opposite is often all it takes to make that creepy guy go elsewhere.

We have been endowed with certain inalienable rights — as citizens, and as Mother Nature's creatures, too. We suggest that you work on catching yourself when you try to talk yourself out of a gut feeling. Your gut is on *your* side. Later you can ask yourself, "was I over-reacting?" But respond first, analyze later... just like the deer in the forest.

BETTY BOO!

The aunt of one of our high school students had taken our class in the early 90s. For this story, we'll call her Beijing Betty. She was thrilled and honored to have been selected as a delegate to the United Nations Fourth World Conference on Women, held in Beijing, China, in the late summer of 1995. She was also a journalist, and had successfully jumped through the numerous, time-consuming hoops that both the People's Republic of China and the United Nations had rigged up to keep just anyone from getting press credentials. A relatively recent graduate of IMPACT Personal Safety's entire curriculum, she felt newly empowered to be an international traveler and reporter. All she needed was a fedora and belted raincoat to complete the picture.

The Chinese government clamped down on the

eve of the Women's conference. They made it a crime for a Chinese citizen to even *speak* to a delegate or a journalist, and they searched the bags of visitors for outlawed books. They also apparently trained thousands of amateur "gumshoes" — an old-fashioned name for private detectives — to tail foreign journalists to make sure they didn't talk to a regular Chinese citizen.

Such was the climate surrounding Betty when she found herself in China, and it only got worse. She went back to her room one afternoon and caught a man rifling through her bags. The second she opened the door, he ran out. The hairs went up on the back of her neck when she knew absolutely that she was being monitored.

The next day, Betty stepped off the bus and prepared her notebook and briefcase while juggling her umbrella, since it was raining, and prepared to walk several blocks in order to visit a new department store that was being heralded as proof of the "people's" progress. She started walking and within moments smelled the combined stench of powerful body odor and really strong, cheap tobacco. She turned around, saw a man duck into an alleyway, and realized she was most likely being followed. Betty was also glad she had a "nose" for trouble... the man reeked!

Her adrenaline surged, and she recognized from her adrenaline-state training at IMPACT that she felt threatened. She consciously made herself breathe and slow down. Betty then decided that she needed to confirm her suspicion, rather than feel like she was just letting her imagination run wild. After all, the delegation and press had heard about the government crackdown of citizens trying to talk to journalists. Betty did not want to inadvertently get an innocent person in trouble by asking the man if he was following her, so she was going out of her way to not be seen speaking to a Chinese citizen, even for directions.

She crossed the street. The "spy" crossed the street. She stopped. He stopped. She lingered at a window and looked into the reflection. She saw him whip out a newspaper, pretend to read it and then glance at her. If it weren't so nerve-wracking, it would have been like a G-rated kids' comedy version of a spy thriller. But images of Chinese prisons wafted through Betty's mind, based on the Amnesty International reports she had read before leaving, so she took the situation seriously.

Betty finally reached the department store. Thinking quickly, she decided to trap the man if she could. How to prove that he was up to no good? "Aha!"

Betty thought, "I have the perfect idea." She rode the escalator up to the second floor, glanced around and spotted what she wanted — the ladies lingerie department! Presumably, most men would not follow an unknown woman into such an area.

She went up to the wall that had bras hanging in neat rows by color. She fingered the fabric on the cups. She worked her way over to the full length mirror so she could hold a bra up to her chest as well as get a rearview look at Mr. Awesomely Bad Detective. Sure enough, as soon as she looked in the mirror, she saw him lift up a camera, prepared to take a shot.

She turned around in a split-second and yelled "Boo!" Inspector Clueless screamed, dropped his camera, turned heel and ran out. He did not get his picture.

Note to Chinese government: The Acme Spy School's 2-Day Guide For Teaching Espionage To Surveillance Wannabes apparently didn't factor in dealing with women who actually know a thing or two about protecting themselves!

HOW WE SEE IT

"BOO!!" Ahhh, we are still laughing about the detective screaming like a little boy. The gumshoe-wannabe needs to go back to school; can you imagine the old, bad detective films he must have watched to get his ideas? Come on: stopping when she stops, pretending to read a newspaper, how else could he come up with such amazingly ineffective subterfuge? Guess he didn't know who he was dealing with in this intrepid reporter!

Beijing Betty did a great job of handling this situation on many levels. Betty was thoughtful in her decision-making, not wanting to draw the attention and possible ire of authorities onto the Chinese citizen and possibly getting an innocent man in trouble. But she knew from the very beginning that something was wrong. She knew from the moment she smelled the body odor and stale cigarette smoke, and saw the little man ducking into an alleyway. Betty's intuition was working full-bore and she was paying attention.

On some levels, having caught the other man rifling through her things was useful to Betty. It caused her to be more aware and it proved that the rumors they were hearing about the Chinese Government and their tactics were indeed true.

We have visions of Lois Lane — IMPACT trained of course — rushing across the street in her smart outfit and matching trench coat with note pad in hand, not shying away from danger but confronting it on her own terms. What better place for this woman to deal with a dangerous man than a stereotypical female-only milieu: the department store?

Once the little man entered the lingerie department, Betty knew she had him; her choice of responses is one that will have a little place in our hearts forever. "BOO!"

B is for BOUNDARIES

Boundaries, simply put, are limits. Here's a startling statistic and one we want you to grapple with. Contrary to what the media and pop culture would have you believe, for the most part women and kids are *not* assaulted by strangers! In the majority of cases, women and kids are assaulted by *someone they know*. These are typically family members, relatives, or people in authority who are known to the victims. Yes, we talk about defending against strangers, and it's our ardent wish that you translate what we teach you into defending yourself against assault from *anyone*, whether you know the person or not.

Because our understanding of boundaries is learned as children in an informal way, most of us are not sure what rights we have when it comes to telling people what we want... or more often, *don't* want. We were taught to respect our elders and do as they say, even when it felt icky. How many of us learned that we had the right to set boundaries and have them respected? How many of us learned that it's okay for us to say "no" when we mean no, and "yes" when we mean yes? Instead, most of us learned to respond or act in a way that pleases the other person. And this is especially true in matters of the heart.

Boundaries, simply put, are lines that mark or define limits. Therefore personal boundaries can be used to set personal limits. These limits can be physical, emotional, or verbal with the people we interact with, whether strangers, friends, family members, or authority figures.

It's an old cliché that when women say "no," they really mean "yes." The reason clichés exist is that they have elements of truth to them. Women have the bad reputation, especially in matters of intimacy, for saying "no" and then letting themselves be manipulated into saying "yes." We do this for various reasons. One of the most prevalent is that we want people to like us, especially those to whom we are attracted. A girl or woman is more likely to say yes to intimacy for which she is not ready, than to say no and risk the boy or man no longer liking her.

Red Alert! Battle Stations! If the guy is basing his part of the relationship on whether you will have sex with him on the first date or not, then good riddance! Bye-bye, so long, farewell. Although this is often easier said than done, it still needs to be said.

One thing to remember is that yes and no are not the only choices we have. We suggest saying "maybe" when you are not sure. For example, in an intimate situation, if you like the person but are not ready to go to the next step, just say so and be straightforward. "I really like you, but I'm not ready to go to the next level. I'm afraid that if I say 'no' you won't like me anymore, but I'm hoping you are the guy I think you are and will take some time and build a relationship with me." Wow! That was clear and to the point, right?

Sex is all around us. It's in movies, on TV, the Internet, in just about every advertisement you have ever seen, it's in our faces at school all day long… and yet, we are uncomfortable talking about it with someone we are considering having an intimate relationship with. What's up with that?

The good thing about this is that boundaries are not set in stone; we can decide what our personal boundaries are for us right now, today. We then are free to loosen boundaries when *we* feel like it. We can start setting boundaries with the people in our lives right now... even with people we never set limits with before! We can learn to set boundaries in a safe and comfortable way, so that we get our needs met without alienating the people in our lives. The more we practice telling people what we want and being clear about our needs, the easier this will become day by day — and then, by extension, in a crisis situation.

Setting limits — boundaries — with people you think might cause you harm can also be instructive, as their response is a useful potential problem gauge. For instance, if you set a boundary with someone and they disrespect or completely ignore your request, you have a clear indication that the person with whom you are dealing is going to be a problem.

Example: If a stranger is "invading your space" and you say, "Sir, back up, you're too close," and he continues to close in on your personal space, you know there's now a problem. What? Are you thinking, "Oh, I could *never* say something like that to a stranger." We think you can, and should, especially if you know you have the right to do it. And we also know that practicing saying what you want makes it easier.

Finally, setting boundaries with loved ones can be *really* hard, even harder than with strangers. Recent brain science has explored the power of oxytocin, which some researchers have nicknamed "the friend and befriend hormone." Simply put, oxytocin is a bonding chemical that is released when you are happy or have had a good experience with someone. If you've bonded with someone — and frequently a sexual experience will release oxytocin — your body will want to override what even common sense says is not good for you. Just being aware of the power of oxytocin can help you set boundaries with people you are attracted to, but intellectually know aren't interested in for your long term well-being.

For friends and family members who are getting on your nerves, or with whom you need to set a boundary, we've got a special boundary-setting tool that is really helpful — perhaps even magical — which is why we call it the **Magic Formula**. And here it is:

"I feel... when you... would you please..."

Here's how it works. Let's say your friend Sheri has a really annoying habit of finishing your sentences for you. It's so hard to think, when she finishes so many of your sentences, that you feel like just shutting up and not working so hard to be heard.

We recommend that you say, "Sheri, **I feel** anxious and frustrated **when you** finish most of my sentences. **Would you please** stop interrupting, and allow me to finish before you speak?

If Sheri responds by saying, "But you're so slow! And I always know what you're going to say anyway," you might want to reassess your relationship. A real friend will say, "I didn't realize I was doing that! And I had no idea you felt badly when I did. I won't do it anymore." A truly dear friend will add, "Thank you for telling me. Is there anything else?"

Boundary setting is one of the best things you can do for yourself and those around you. Not only is it a key element in personal safety, it's a key element in life.

CHARLIE IN CHARGE

You've just entered the workforce in a big way, by getting an internship at a big office. It's intimidating at first and then you relax. But you also begin to notice some office politics and ways that people speak to each other that make you feel bad. What will you do? Check out Charlie's approach…

Charlie had been a paralegal for many years. She had earned her stripes with an elite Los Angeles law firm after working on the infamous MGM Grand Hotel fire case in the early 1980s. She was no greenhorn, which is an old-fashioned term for "newbie." She knew her way around the office and the courtroom. Years later, once she had children, she decided to take a job closer to home in a small Southern California town. No one who knew Charlie was surprised when she took charge and had things running more efficiently within a few short months.

Not long after, the firm hired a new attorney — let's call him "James" — from a fancy-schmancy law firm in New York. Just her luck, she thought. Now she was going to have to show James the intricacies of California law, and that would not be fun when the new hire thought he knew more than she.

Unfortunately, James was a jerk. Charlie had no problem handling the arrogant twit; she'd cut her teeth on tougher skin than his. But the bigger problem was that James the Jerk kept upsetting the secretaries and clerks, making any number of them cry each day. Charlie could not have that in her office, and decided to do something about it.

Charlie invited all the secretaries and clerks to attend a "filing seminar" at lunch time. Of course no attorney would ever show up for such a topic, so she would be free to say whatever she wanted. As the staff gathered, Charlie let them vent and air their complaints. She heard things like, "He yells at me when I don't do something fast enough," "James calls me Little Miss Snooty," "He looks at my chest the whole time he talks to me," "He called me stupid," and on it went. After she'd heard enough, Charlie said, "Ladies, we have some work to do!" and began to plot out her scheme for the group. Everyone left the "filing seminar" in high spirits with a new mission at hand.

That afternoon the fun began!

Cathy Clerk went into James the Jerk's office with the files he requested. As soon as he began to berate her as expected, she interrupted him. "Excuse me, James, I don't appreciate your tone of voice. I'm going to leave and when you are ready to speak to me respectfully, I will be happy to come back and finish with you." She turned and walked out, closing the door gently behind her. The whole office was silent, waiting to see what would happen next. After about five minutes, James buzzed Cathy and politely asked her to come to his office. She went in, finished her work with him and walked out of the office with a smile on her face; it was all the others could do to not break into a cheer when she came out.

It continued like that for a while, secretaries and clerks setting boundaries and politely walking out of his office, returning after a short "time out." Charlie kept watch on things so it didn't get out of hand, as she didn't want it to backfire. And then, one day the vigilance paid off; you could feel the shift in the office. It took about two weeks, but James began to treat the other people at the law firm with the respect they deserved.

You see, the "filing seminar" was not just a complaint session; it was a boundary-setting and verbal strategy workshop. Charlie had taken an IMPACT class years before and knew the skills she had learned would be helpful here. She dug out her *Women's Basics Course Workbook* from class and put together a lesson plan. She had everyone get up and practice, repeatedly, what they would say to James the Jerk when he was disrespectful. She had them draw on incidents that had already happened, and then had them practice the appropriate boundary-setting response that had evaded them at the time.

Charlie stressed that it was important in this situation to be respectful at all times so James could not complain about them. She had them check in with her each time they set a boundary with James, or when they needed to practice, or even if they needed a shot of courage to stand up to him. She was like the momma bear teaching her cubs to defend themselves… she was so proud!

Months later, at the holiday party, James approached Charlie and said, "I know it was you behind all that 'I don't appreciate your tone of voice' stuff…"

"Yep," Charlie replied, "I don't let *anyone* mess with my firm!"

HOW WE SEE IT

Charlie demonstrated what we like to call the "collateral benefits" of effective self-defense training. When most people think of self-defense training, they naturally and automatically think about the most dramatic application: defense against a mugging or other crime attempt. But we hear time and time again about the not-so-obvious "fallout" from learning how to set and maintain boundaries physically. We hear of students who find a new level of self-esteem from experiencing their ability to defend themselves, and that esteem can translate into the workplace or home. Things that had previously intimidated, or even petrified them before the self-defense class ceased to frighten them after. We know of people who have asked for long overdue promotions, or who have asked a loved one to stop talking to them in a particular tone that had been hurtful.

Charlie was able to translate what she learned about setting verbal boundaries into a workplace that depended on her eyes, ears and brains for a well-functioning law firm.

Not a lot of people know how the paralegal staff is the invisible and essential part of such a firm. Charlie knew that if her staff was unhappy, the lawyers — and by extension, clients — would suffer as a result.

Charlie was smart because, even though people might hate being talked down to, there are very few examples of successfully altering bad behavior in a person with more clout. Just think of the times you may have muttered or complained to someone else about "What I could have/ should have said," but came up short in the moment. Your inability to say something in the moment is probably due to the chemical spill that happens when you feel threatened: adrenalin, and then cortisol, surge in our bodies even if it's merely words that are being hurled at us. Even though James the Jerk wasn't necessarily threatening the office staff physically, he was dominating them with his rude and crude actions and words. The implied threat was, there could be consequences in standing up to someone who could have you fired for insubordination. The women working for him knew that if they complained, it would probably end up in a "He said, she said" situation, or "I was just joking! Why can't you women take a joke," or "Why didn't you complain to me at the time?"

In hierarchically-run businesses, it's particularly challenging — short of a formal complaint or even a lawsuit — to impact higher-ups with jerk attitudes and actions. James the Jerk had apparently gotten away with bullying in his previous environments.

Take note! You could save your company or firm a lot of lost hours, and potentially the cost of a harassment suit, if you could send all the employees through a self-defense program that includes *verbal* self-defense training.

Charlie had the office staff practice. In order to override their adrenalin, she had them do "rehearsals" of what they would say the next time he spoke to them disrespectfully. Charlie knew he would give them ample opportunities to test their new-found skills. He was not going to change on his own.

Sure enough, Charlie not only changed James the Jerk's behavior but altered the culture of the firm itself. She stuck her neck out, but we're positive that the women who worked for her were not only able to set boundaries with employers, but were most likely able to take their skills back into their homes and to pass on what they learned to their kids. Bad behavior may be contagious but so is good behavior. We are *firmly* behind Charlie and her commitment to the entire staff's well-being. We think they should have made her a partner.

C is for COURAGE

Amelia Earhart, the famous aviator, knew a thing or two about courage. In the early part of the 20th Century, she flew when most women and girls were convinced that flying airplanes was a "male only" pursuit. Indeed, adventure was considered to be too dangerous for females. So Earhart not only had to conquer the natural fear of learning something new — even though she had dreamed of flight since she first saw an airplane flying over her as a young girl — but she had to fight the fear of stretching beyond societal limits. She wrote in a poem:

> Courage is the price that life exacts for granting peace.
> The soul that knows it not, knows no release
> From little things;
> Knows not the livid loneliness of fear,
> Nor mountain heights where bitter joy can hear
> The sound of wings.

Our *Charlie in Charge* story exemplifies the courage to lead, to notice what needs to be changed and then to take charge.

In order to grow, we must employ courage. While courage itself can't be taught, we can *encourage* you to have it. The word "courage" comes from the French word "coeur" for "heart." If you are discouraged, you are down-hearted. When we encourage each other, we truly give one another heart, another way of saying "strength." Self-defense — whether it's verbal or physical — draws on your courage, your strength.

We write about courage in this personal safety book because every time we teach a class, we see courage. The students need courage for a wide spectrum of actions: sometimes that can be as simple as finally being able to say "No" for the first time to someone who is bothering them.

Courage is not the absence of fear, as many people think, but taking action *regardless* of the fear. You can see how some people spend a lifetime waiting to fulfill their dreams, believing they must first overcome their fear before venturing into something they dream of doing. They don't realize that fear is *always* with us! The key is not to ignore it, but instead take it with you... make friends with it.

It's the people who say, "I am afraid, but I'm forging ahead anyway" who know what courage is. It takes courage to learn how to defend yourself. Like Amelia Earhart, even if you have the desire to learn to defend yourself, there's a large social factor that says "Girls can't fight back. Don't try. Boys don't like girls who are strong. You'll just make things worse if you fight back."

Then you might have an inner doubting voice that says, "What if I get hurt? What will people think of me? Will I be made fun of? Will I fail?"

These are all perfectly normal thoughts. And if you look at it, they are similar to thoughts you probably had when you learned *anything* new, right? If you have a pulse, which we know you do because you're reading this, you're going to resist being a beginner at most things. Relax. It's OK.

Don't let other people discourage you. They are often merely projecting their own fears on you, like you're some type of mirror. Their fear can pull you down. We've also noticed that fear can be contagious. If you grow up in a household that emphasizes that the world is full of "scary" things or situations, yet offers no solutions to deal with them, fears will grow to the point where they can immobilize you. The irony here is the fear mongers think they are protecting you. There's a saying, "Ignorance is bliss." We think ignorance is not bliss, but instead terrifying.

That's the bad news. But here's the good news:

The Safety Godmothers believe that courage is also contagious and worth spreading. When you are courageous, you like yourself more. You could say that we are in the courage business. Even though it sounds silly to say that we serve courage in every class, it's nonetheless true.

Eleanor Roosevelt, a First Lady of the United States and an incredibly courageous woman, said, "We gain strength, and courage, and confidence by each experience in which we really stop to look fear in the face... we must do that which we think we cannot." She also said, "do one thing every day that scares you."

If your first reaction to self-defense is fear, that's fine: admit it and face it. We're here to help you. Then step up and do the thing that scares you. You'll like yourself more each time you do!

DENISE DOWN FRONT

Denise loved Coachella! She loved the bands, the crowds and the heat. Denise was in the middle of her high school IMPACT class when the wildly popular annual Coachella Music Festival began. For those who don't know what Coachella is, it's a huge outdoor music festival on the west coast.

Denise was secretly happy she had taken the class, because she almost always was involved in — or witnessed — uncomfortable situations in the desert. Her parents were not-so-secretly happy she was taking the self-defense class, too; they always got anxious when she went to Coachella, and this year her brother was not going along. She would be on her own for the first time.

Denise was swaying to the music of Smashing Pumpkins when the guy behind her — who had been sending out a noticeable alcohol breeze — reached around and grabbed her breasts. She took hold of his hands, turned around, looked him in the eye and said, "keep your hands off of me" and went back to listening to the music. Seconds later, the same thing happened again. This time, she grabbed his hands with more force, added a little twist and said, "I mean it. Keep your hands off of me or there will be trouble."

The jerk behind her chuckled at her threat and reached around and grabbed her breasts one more time. Denise reached out in front of her with her right arm to set up the strike, then swiftly swung back with an elbow strike that met its mark. She hit him right in the nose with her elbow; she not only felt the nose break, but she heard it, too.

Denise heard the crowd around her cheering, but it had nothing to do with the music — it was in response to her actions! Next, the crowd picked up the attacker and passed him over their heads to the security guards on the perimeter. She never saw him again.

HOW WE SEE IT

The problem with events like this is that people think all bets are off and inappropriate behavior is acceptable. It's not. For too long we, as a society, have let "little annoyances" slip by without consequence and because of this, the inappropriate behavior escalates.

We are pretty sure this weasel has done it before, and gotten away with his bad behavior over and over again. It's likely no one confronted him for his actions, which were just written off with comments like, "boys will be boys" or "he was just joking around." But we often don't speak up because we don't want to appear rude, or make the other person uncomfortable, or be seen as someone who causes trouble, or someone who has no "sense of humor," or whatever lame societal excuses we use.

When a situation like this comes up, what **the Safety Godmothers** want you to ask yourself is "Why is it okay for *me* to be uncomfortable, but not the person who is ignoring my boundary? Why is it okay for this person to grab me or scare me, but it's not okay for me to confront him?" We think you have the right to stand up for yourself, anytime you want, for any reason you want. And we firmly believe that, if we continue to set boundaries and teach other people to do so as well, it will be more acceptable to be polite and friendly than rude and inappropriate. What a novel concept!

We also want to point out that Denise gave the miscreant two chances to stop: she also clearly warned him there would be trouble if he continued, but he did not respect her or her wishes. **The Safety Godmothers** know that situations like this only spiral out of control: if she had let the dolt get away with the groping, we are certain he would have continued on to more inappropriate behavior and possibly become dangerous. We are also pretty sure that, after his interaction with Denise, he won't be letting his fingers do the walking ever again!

D is for the 4D'S OF BOUNDARY SETTING

What are the "4D's"?

- Distance
- Dynamics
- Dissuasion
- Don't Back Up / Don't Back Down

We call them the 4D's as a mnemonic device to help you remember what to look for in a potential confrontation. Technically there are 5D's, but we count the two D's in "Don't Back Up / Don't Back Down" as the 4th D. When you are in an uncertain situation, you can use the 4D template to help you determine what is going on in the circumstances that feel threatening; this in turn can lead to ideas for how you want to handle yourself and the other person.

We just want to be clear about one thing before we dive into the 4D's; you already know what to do when everything is fine, when there is no threat or concern about your safety. If it seems like things are normal, you just go about things in your normal way. The 4D's are for when your intuition (see *I is for Intuition*) perks up and tells you to be alert. If you continue to hone your awareness and intuition skills, which are your first lines of defense, you do not have to walk through your life on red alert; your survival instincts will tell you when you should employ the 4D's.

There's a pattern with the first three of the D's. In each case, there's a question you ask yourself to help you assess the situation and decide on your strategy.

The first question — Distance: "How close do I let a stranger get?"

We suggest two arm's lengths distance + a little bit more between you and someone about whom you are uncertain. Don't be afraid to set and maintain a safe boundary distance. If the person in question is close enough to touch you, he is too close. Remember that he can close the distance between himself and you very quickly.

Human reaction time is about ¼ of a second. That means it takes the body about ¼ of a second to respond to what the brain tells it to do. When the assailant is one arms' length, or less, away from you, you are in the danger zone. With that distance, if he tries to grab or hit you, you do not have enough time to react effectively. However, when the assailant is two arms' length, or more, away — a safe distance — if he tries to grab or hit, he has to take a step in and you have the time to react. So, as a general rule, we believe a two arms' length distance is the closest you want a stranger to be, especially those that set off your internal alarm system.

We know this distance is not realistic for day-to-day living; we all have to wait in lines, ride the bus, and spend time in close situations. What we want you to remember is when people are close to you, keep your awareness up, trust your instincts about people, and increase your distance as a means of staying safe. If you are concerned about hurting the person's feelings, ask yourself which is more important: your safety or his feelings. We say your safety is *always* the priority.

The Safety Godmothers would like you to actually practice saying, "You're a little close. Could you please back up?" For many of us, that is hard to say at first. If you are one of those people, that is a good indicator of why it's important to learn to say it with a straight face. You have every right to request a distance that feels comfortable to you.

Technically speaking, the farther you are from danger the better. If you get a "funny" feeling about something or someone, cross the street, turn around and leave, don't get on the elevator with them, do whatever you need to do in order not to be there. A colleague of ours, Cliff Stewart, terms this kind of action, "target denial" because we're actively not providing a target.

The Second Question — Dynamics: "What is going on here?"

What are the dynamics here? Every situation is different. Awareness is extremely important; you must know what is going on around you. What is the intent of the other person? What does your intuition say? Are you in danger, or is he just asking for the time? Is he actually close enough to do something or is he a block away? If it is an assault, what is happening with this person who's attempting a possible assault?

What's going on with him; what are his personal dynamics? Is he…
- Angry?
- Crazy?
- Creepy?
- Drunk / On Drugs?
- Nervous?
- Suave? (Is he actively "charming" or conning me?)

And what's going on with me?
- How do I feel?
- Am I doubting myself?

- How am I dressed? Can I kick these shoes off or are they strapped on with a buckle?
- Am I injured or impaired?
- What's going on around us?
- Where is safety?
- Are there people around?
- Can someone help me?

It's grounding and calming to ask yourself these questions instead of immediately assuming the worst or staying with the freeze response.

The Third Question — Dissuasion: "How am I going to talk him out of it?"

Let's, for the sake of this conversation, determine that you believe an assault is about to happen. Human beings have a powerful tool for defense: their language and speaking, which can be far more effective than force. We want to get you used to the idea of asking yourself, "What can I do or say that will convince him I am a bad choice for an assault?" If it is an assault, the first line of defense should be dissuasion, if possible. The goal is to calm him down, divert, or discourage the attack. Escalation and a show of stance could make things worse when you engage his ego and make it hard for him to simply walk away. This is where your verbal strategies come in: they are key to self-defense.

For instance, if he is angry, you *always* want to de-escalate. *Do not* have a conversation with a man who is yelling at you — or a woman, for that matter; yelling back will only escalate the situation. Leave your ego behind and let them have the last word. Let them insult you as long as you've stopped their assault. (*For more ideas, see "V is for Verbal Strategies."*)

Now that the questions are answered and the situation is clear, it's time for the 4th D:

Don't Back Up / Don't Back Down — "Once you have drawn the line, stand your ground."

Don't be driven backward by him: this gives him power and puts you at a disadvantage! Once you decide you have no other choice, once you realize you cannot get away, you must stand your ground both physically and verbally.

Many states have a "stand your ground" law. Many of us weren't aware of this until the infamous 2012 "Trayvon Martin" case in Florida, which involved firearms. However, the primary intent of these laws has nothing to do with weapons. For example, in the state of California you have the legal right to stand your ground and to strike the first blow if you feel your life is in imminent danger. You must find out what laws your state has relating to self-defense in these types of situations.

When it comes to IMPACT and our training, standing your ground is not just a slogan. The type of defense we employ is "defensive counter-attack," and these techniques do not work as well if you are moving backward. By the same token, you don't need to defend yourself if the assailant is running away! In nearly every effective defense situation, once the "action" starts you must be moving forward. The assailant is only drawn in and gains more momentum if you are moving backward.

If you say there will be consequences, you must deliver them. For example, you say assertively, "If you take one more step, I will yell for help," giving him one more chance to walk away. Then, if he doesn't walk away, you must immediately call for help so he knows you will do what you said you'd do.

Additionally, body language is very important to the 4D's and to successful self-defense. How you present yourself physically is actually in many ways more powerful than your words. The idea is to look and sound like a *bad target*. Here are some specifics on how to do that:

Congruent/ Strong Body Language	Incongruent/ Weak Body Language
Good posture	Slouching
Eye contact	Looking away
Steady footwork	Moving feet too much
Solid stance	Head down
Being relaxed	Miscellaneous nervous habits

If we look at the story *Denise Down Front*, we can see the 4D's at work. Denise was not able to keep a two arms' length **distance** between her and anyone in the mosh pit, but she was aware of the people around her. It was clear what was going on, and she understood the **dynamics** of the situation: people were drinking and dancing and generally not paying attention to the boundaries of others. Denise knew right away that the guy groping her was drunk because he reeked of booze. She also knew that she was on her own in that sea of people. No one else was going to stand up for her at that moment, so she took the situation into her own hands. After her first request was ignored, Denise — using **dissuasion** — gave a direct order to stop and said there would be consequences if he did not comply. Finally, she did not **back up**, nor did she **back down** from her direct order; she gave him two chances to stop and when he did not, she delivered her consequence… pow! Right in the kisser!

The 4D's are simple, common sense tools that you can use to assess and successfully handle many dangerous or uncomfortable situations, and can be used both with people you know or with strangers. They are very handy… learn them and you'll experience a new level of personal confidence.

ELISE ELEVATOR

Elise was anxious to get home. She'd spent most of a long day pitching an idea to a big downtown LA company, and decided to have tea and wait out the traffic before she hit the road. She was not eager to be at the back end of a bunch of cars billowing exhaust. She stepped onto the elevator and a young man in a business suit eyed her. He reeked of English Leather. Elise remembered thinking, "That's odd… why is a relatively young guy wearing his father's 70s-era cologne?"

The office was on the 30th floor and Elise looked up at the numbers, the way we all look at the numbers so we don't have to look at, or speak to, people on an elevator. English Leather Guy cleared his throat and said, "You have a beautiful body." What?! This was completely unexpected and utterly out of the blue. Elise tightly said, "OK, thanks," and went back to looking at the numbers, thinking her obviously terse tone would set a boundary. He again cleared his throat and said, "Can't you take a compliment? You're so pretty. Why the ugly look on your face?"

The hairs on the back of Elise's neck stood up. She cleared *her* throat this time and said, "Oh, yes… well, it's just that I feel really guilty about a man I beat up once in an elevator. He was in the hospital for 2 months. He had it coming, but I still feel guilty."

English Leather Guy immediately pushed the button for the next floor and virtually sprinted off the elevator a nanosecond after the doors opened… and didn't look back.

HOW WE SEE IT

What is it Gavin de Becker says in his bestseller, *The Gift of Fear*, about elevators? We're paraphrasing here: "Humans are the only creatures who will step into a soundproof metal box that has only one escape route with a person who makes them uncomfortable, just so they don't make the *other* person feel awkward." Crazy, isn't it? You're going to put yourself right into the line of danger while listening to your intuition scream at you that something is wrong and ignoring it, just so you're not rude to this guy who you think might attack you right here and now? And he's also someone you may never see again! It happens all of the time.

But it didn't happen to Elise! She knew as soon as she smelled the aftershave that something was off. She joked with herself about him wearing his father's cologne from the 70s, but the dark humor was really her intuition drawing facts together to alert her. That's not to say some really nice guys don't wear stinky cologne revered by men from the Bronze Age, but the smell tipped her off and shifted her intuition into gear.

The "compliment" itself was not the worst of it, though there are more respectful and appropriate ways to flatter a person. But the way he reacted to her response was The Big Reveal. A well-meaning man would have apologized for being so forward as soon as he saw her discomfort; this guy not only enjoyed it, he even tried to increase her uneasiness by using a tactic called "Typecasting," also eloquently described in *The Gift of Fear*. By saying "Can't you take a compliment? You're so pretty. Why the ugly look on your face?" he was manipulating her to convince him that she *could* take a compliment and that she was *not* ugly and thus engaging her in a longer conversation.

But again, Elise did not fall for the ploy. She was able to keep her wits about her and respond effectively while adrenalized, thanks to her previous training. Elise turned the tables on creepy old, er, young, English Leather Guy and he skittered away, just like the coward we thought he was!

E is for EGO (and ESTEEM)

Egos are important; we all have them. Egos are part and parcel of healthy personal psychology. They allow us to say "Ouch" when something hurtful has happened. On the other hand, unhealthy or out of balance egos can also get us in trouble, or cause trouble for others. One of the other important "E" words is "esteem"; as you'll see, ego and esteem are linked.

Elise Elevator used an ego-based defense: boasting about something she'd never done in order to puff herself up and deflate English Leather guy. She inflated herself to make him afraid of her! She used his ego against him.

A major factor in socializing girls, and then women, is to emphasize "niceness" as a virtue. Many women and girls tend to build character "capital" and esteem by being nice, no matter what. **The Safety Godmothers** like nice, so don't get us wrong: we're not advocating that people *not* be nice. What we *do* advocate is to have people use the tool "nice" when it's appropriate, and to also practice the "not nice" tools when appropriate. Unfortunately, the desire to be friendly — another form of nice — can put girls and women in danger.

Another form of socialization is to validate boys who go after what they want, without hindering them, which can create bullying in extreme situations. Healthy boys and girls find an ego and esteem balance that help them grow into healthy adults.

Too often, girls and women hide their real thoughts, or will not set a boundary with someone for fear of not being liked or having people think they're a "bitch," the opposite of nice. For example, many assault survivors will say they knew something was wrong with the person or the situation, but didn't speak up because they thought it wasn't nice to even *have* those thoughts, or that they were "being silly." A similar refrain is they didn't want to appear rude or to hurt that person's feelings. But the fact is the potential assailant doesn't care one bit about your well being, so why would you care whether they like you or not, or that they called you a bitch? So what? (For an entire rant on the word "Bitch," see Chapter 11 of *Beauty Bites Beast: Awakening The Warrior Within Women And Girls,* Safety Godmother Ellen Snortland's book about her experience of IMPACT Personal Safety. A condensed version appears at www.snortland.com/PW-3-1-08.html)

Setting a boundary is a good way to find out the essential goodness of a person. If they respect the boundary you set, they are in the "good" camp; i.e., if you set a boundary with a well-meaning person, they may not like it, but they will not assault you for it. If you set a boundary with someone whose intent is malicious, they will continue to push and disrespect you and your efforts to set limits. This is a **RED FLAG**, whether it's a prospective date or a possible assailant on the street. Good people respect boundaries, and bad people don't. Sorry to be so black and white about it, but the gray areas of boundaries are cleared up by communicating what your boundary is. You can only set a boundary when your ego and self-esteem are strong enough to do so.

Do not base your ego on whether people think you're nice or not. Instead, try being proud of your intuition. If your intuition tells you something is wrong, *something is wrong.* If you trust your instincts and stop trying to be friendly to everyone and anyone, you might save your life. And in daily matters, you most certainly will gain respect, from your friends and yourself… a much better deal in the long run.

Ego is also what drives most assailants; they lack self-confidence and self-esteem and they make themselves feel better by hurting someone they perceive as weaker than themselves. They feed their own egos by preying upon people whom they think will not put up a fight. If you think about it in this light, the scary person may only be covering up how insecure they feel. Not that scary then, right?

The assailant, of whom we are afraid, is such a coward that he must choose a prospective victim based solely upon whether he perceives he can win or not. Mr. Assailant does not go looking for the strongest, most confident person he can find. A healthy ego would determine that someone looking for a real challenge would find someone who is as strong or stronger then they are.

This puts a potential victim at a psychological advantage for several reasons: you know from the very beginning that this guy, this potential assailant, has no confidence and is a coward at heart; if you move through the world with confidence and awareness, you will not be perceived as weak and therefore not a good target; and if they do confront you, simple verbal strategies will most likely make him flee to find easier "hunting." Strong, confident men do not attack women or children or even other men; they find other outlets to deal with the needs of their egos.

Playground and workplace bullies are also cowards at heart. Most bullies did not get the attention or ego-stroking that we all need as kids and therefore have a screwed-up way of proving themselves. In most cases, bullies fashion themselves after an adult of influence in their lives and are not taught how to interact with other people in healthy ways. They do not learn how to lose graciously, take "no" for an answer, or even how to take even the simplest of rejections or kindest criticism. Their only way of working out disagreements or dealing with not getting their way is to force people — to bully them — into agreement.

Healthy egos and balanced self-esteem are psychological vitamin "E"s and are needed every day to stay emotionally and physically safe from the people who have an "E" deficiency.

FRANK FRAPPUCCINO

Frank was in the grocery store with his mom for their weekly shopping trip in their upscale neighborhood in Los Angeles, California. He was 10 and he'd rather have been with his friends, but he didn't mind so much since his mom often let him get a Frappuccino with no coffee from the in-store Starbucks.

As he stood in line at Starbucks, he noticed a woman around his grandmother's age hanging around the edges of the café. His parents had enrolled him in the IMPACT Kids' self-defense class about three years earlier, so — when his intuition told him something was wrong — instead of ignoring or denying it, he paid attention. He knew that his intuition was a very good friend.

Sure enough, once he gave the barista his order, the older woman walked up to him and said "Hey, little boy, I already have one of those tall mocha Frappuccinos with no coffee in my car. You can have it if you want."

Frank was not falling for that! He turned toward the woman in ready stance with his hands up and said "No! I don't take bribes, ma'am, and if you don't leave right now, I will call security!"

The woman looked surprised and mumbled something about "… didn't mean anything … don't have to tell anyone …" as she quickly walked away.

As soon as the barista came back to the counter, Frank told her what happened and she called security. She also gave him his drink for free for doing such a good job of setting boundaries!

HOW WE SEE IT

Frank did everything exactly the way he learned in his kids' personal safety class. He listened to his inner voice which told him something was not right, and then he acted on it. This makes **The Safety Godmothers** *very* happy!

He said "No!" which is the first line of verbal defense for anyone, regardless of age. Saying "No!" out loud serves several purposes: it gets the person who is saying or yelling "No!" focused and breathing; it alerts other people who may be around that something is happening that at least one of the participants doesn't want; it puts the potential assailant on alert that this is not going to be an easy attack. See how useful the word "No!" can be?

He then informed the woman that he doesn't take bribes. Frank was taught in his class that it's important to not take anything from someone he doesn't know, even if it's a gift. Why would someone Frank doesn't know offer him anything? Adults who are truly "child friendly" know not to offer kids things to eat or drink. Adults also know to never ask for help from a kid, as in, "My puppy is lost. Can you help me find her?" Grown-ups don't ask kids they don't know to help them out in *any* situation.

There are many basic kids rules, and we'll touch on more of them in other parts of this book. Frank hadn't been in class for 3 years, but just like learning to ride a bike, his safety lessons stayed with him. He practiced them and didn't just talk about them. That's why they stayed with him and he was able to use them when needed.

F is for FEAR

Most of us are raised to avoid fear. As children, our parents protected us from all kinds of things. We got to sleep in our parents' bed when we were afraid at night. We weren't allowed to watch scary movies until we were older. We probably were sheltered from specific information when family members died, like grandparents, etc., because most modern Americans fear death and dying. And most of us are afraid of fear itself. But without fear, we would not recognize danger.

In the story *Frank Frappuccino* we see that while Frank may have been afraid, he was not too fearful to speak up for himself. Rather than just comply with the lady and get duped into getting into her car and ending up who knows where, he stood up for himself. He was able to do that because he had learned in his personal safety class that it was easier to speak up right away than to wait to see what happens. He learned that if he was too afraid of a person to speak up for himself, then he should be even more afraid *not* to do so. Also, he knew the fear was fleeting, and it was a signal to him to take care of himself.

Remember that we talked in previous chapters about how our bodies are designed to keep the body itself alive? And about how we have different systems and mechanisms designed to keep us safe? Fear is one of the most important instruments of our safety. If we didn't feel fear, we would take risks that are unwarranted or needlessly dangerous; without fear, we would not use caution. Fear alerts us, and if we listen to the signal the moment it alerts us, we can avoid the danger altogether.

In Gavin de Becker's book, *The Gift of Fear,* he talks about fear being a survival signal. He says that without fear, we would do some really stupid things. Fear is the chain that yanks us back and says "Whoa, hold on a second…" before we jump off a cliff or do something equally foolhardy.

We, **the Safety Godmothers**, were also raised to fear violence and rightly so, but we believe that all of us give assailants too much credit; that society has learned some fear to its detriment. Men who attack women are cowards. Period. As we discussed in the chapter on "Ego," the men who assault women and children — and this includes bullies — are looking for an easy target.

What most of us don't think about is this: what do the *criminals* fear? What are *they* afraid of?! For the most part, CAPTURE… and that's how we can use their fear against them.

Criminals, and by extension predators in general, flourish when their "prey" stay silent, isolate themselves, or comply. If you are willing to transcend your own fear of making a scene, you will shift the balance of power. When you yell, when you put up a fight, all of a sudden the fear has shifted over to the criminal who is afraid of the ruckus YOU are making getting him in trouble! Fear is not only a gift, as a signal that something is wrong, but fear is your friend because you can turn the tables and make someone afraid of *you*!

What we are trying to get across here is that fear is an important mechanism designed to keep us safe. Healthy fear is good to have; to let fear control our lives is bad.

Finally, what many of us tag as fear is really *worry*. Worry is, excuse the expression, worrisome because worry causes you to be hyper-vigilant about nothing and can wreak havoc with your nervous system. Stop worrying and trust your instincts to let you know when you really need to be afraid. Mother Nature is *very* smart. By trusting yourself, you trust her.

GINA, GIANT SLAYER

Gina was a very petite 17 year old — just 5 feet tall and weighing 100 pounds — when she was accosted outside the grocery store by an older man; a man she thought was finally out of her life. At first, she was swept away by the attentions of Walter — a man 4 years older than Gina and in the military — but the infatuation soon faded when Walter's nasty mean streak and hair-trigger temper made itself evident. Her parents had warned her about Walter, and when Gina finally realized how right they were, she broke up with him.

The day had started out normally, except it was unusual for Gina to dress up. However, this spring morning she felt good and wanted to take advantage of the lovely almost-summer weather. She put on a blue short summer dress and her new kicky, strappy, high heeled sandals and went about her Saturday, a day reserved for chores and errands in her family's household.

Gina's mom had asked her to run some errands, including some light grocery shopping, since Gina now had her driver's license. As she came out of the store, a bag of groceries in each hand, she noticed a very tall man walking quickly toward her. Who he actually was didn't register at first. After all, she hadn't seen her ex-boyfriend since he'd left on his last deployment — after their break-up and the subsequent restraining order — but it was definitely him, all 6' 4" and 200-plus pounds of him.

Without missing a beat, Gina put down the bags, dropped her purse, kicked off her shoes and got into ready stance. "Stop!" she shouted at the top of her lungs, "Walter, do not take another step closer!"

Walter just continued straight toward her, yelling at her the whole time. "You stupid bitch! You think you can just leave me like that? No one leaves me… you are coming back with me!" Gina knew it was time for her to defend herself and did not hesitate. As Walter came barreling toward Gina, she stepped in and heel-palmed him right under the chin. That stopped Walter in his tracks and made him grab his face. As he did so, Gina kneed him in the groin! As his head came down in response to her knee strike, she stepped in and kneed him in the head. Walter went flying backward and hit his head on the ground as he went down, ensuring a good knockout!

The security guard who had shown up just in time to see the knee to the head stood there with his jaw on the ground. "How on earth did a little tiny girl like you do something like *that* to a big guy like him?!" he asked incredulously.

Without answering, Gina grabbed her groceries, purse and sandals (she was not leaving those new sandals behind!) and ran to her car. As she ran, people asked if she was okay. She responded as she kept on moving toward her car, "Yes, I'm fine, please call 911." Once she got into the car, she called her contact at the DA's office and pressed charges against Walter for breaking his restraining order.

HOW WE SEE IT

This is the classic scenario that we practice in the Women's Basics class at IMPACT Personal Safety. Gina did everything she was trained to do. Ready stance, heel palm, knee to the groin, knee to the head, shouting the whole time. She listened to her body and responded. She did not wonder if she was doing the right thing or not. She didn't protect her groceries, her purse or her sandals; she protected herself.

She made a lot of noise; yelling gets your breathing going and also alerts other people to the fact that there's a "scene" happening. And she literally caused a scene; something most women and girls are discouraged to do. Because she made a scene, Walter never bothered her — and hopefully no one else — again. As a matter of fact, his attack landed him in a military brig.

If Gina had followed so-called "conventional wisdom" she would never have even attempted to protect herself against a larger, charging male. Conventional wisdom says "You'll only make him angrier." Really? She used his blind rage against him. Her size, while a factor, did not prevent her from inflicting great damage on him physically, to the point that he was knocked out. So much for his "charge," and so much for conventional wisdom!

Gina may be small in stature, but she is a giant when it comes to fighting spirit. As we say at IMPACT, "It's not the size of the woman in the fight, it's the size of the fight in the woman!"

G is for GIRLS

The Safety Godmothers are here to encourage you to stand up like a girl for what you want. Be proud of your girlhood! But what exactly is a "girl," anyway?

The previous story, *Gina, Giant Slayer*, was a classic David and Goliath tale, famous from the old testament of the Bible. We don't recall anyone doubting that story despite David being small. We *do* run into doubts about girls because there's an accepted yet nonetheless erroneous opinion that girls can't or shouldn't take on a "Goliath."

On its face, "girls" is merely the noun we use for young females. But wait, there's more! Girls can be used as a term of affection between females of any age, up to and including the really old women who play cards with the "girls" at their senior center. On the flip side, girls can be used as a put-down, as in one macho character yelling at another guy he's insulting, "You girls coming with me or not?" as he spits, then revs his engine and leaves the less macho guys in the dust. And the ultimate insult in the military is to call men "girls" or "ladies" (the two words being interchangeable) if they can't keep up.

There are other little digs from men that we hear all the time, in society and the media, like making fun of someone for "running like a girl," or the really annoying one that continually shows up in movies and TV shows where a guy tells another guy "you screamed just like a little girl!" (Don't little boys scream, too? You bet they do!) Then there is the classic sports insult, "You throw like a girl!" You may have seen an artist's answer to that in a poster that's popular with female martial artists: the poster shows a classic judo throw with a girl "thrower" tossing an opponent like a rag doll. The caption is, of course, "Throws Like a Girl" but the visual makes for a delicious twist on that tired phrase.

Calling someone a girl ought to be a compliment and should be used with tones of reverence and awe, and also a way to praise men, not bully them! OK, that might be a bit far-fetched, but maybe not. Let's look at some developments in the visibility and development of the view of girls in the public eye. Never fear, we'll tie this into self-defense by the time we're done.

First, it is important to understand that this "girl" issue really boils down to being a spin problem, one that can affect whether you can get the adults in your school or district to go along with the idea of a self-defense class for girls. Girls are often considered to be incapable, or not as trainable, or less athletic, or inherently not as good at physical things as boys are.

Enter Title IX, which in its simplest form says that if a school receives federal funds for *any* activity, it *must* provide the same opportunities for its girls as it does its boys. The passage of Title IX in 1972 was a veritable boon for young female athletes who had up to that point been basically ignored in favor of all-male football, basketball and baseball teams in their schools. (Bigger schools also had tennis, golf and more, which were almost always populated solely with boys.)

The only real programs for girl athletes used to be gymnastics, softball, cheerleading and maybe the "softer" non-contact sports like swimming and track. Although it's very hard to find a school that has gender equality in terms of facilities, promotion and the same pride in girls' athletic programs as the boys' programs, the situation now — thanks to Title IX

— is *far* better than it used to be. And there's a lot of room to grow. The disparity between athletics programs for boys and girls has a deeper impact on the lives of students, when you consider that participation in athletics not only builds leadership and confidence, but is often the key to winning scholarships and access to higher education that would be otherwise unavailable.

The underlying bias that boys are better than girls is often unconscious, or not openly articulated. Ironically, it is typically the fathers who become champions of their daughters' equal rights in athletic programs. For example, long-time California State Assembly member Anthony Portantino, who in 2012 stepped down to care for his ailing mother, is openly adoring of his two daughters and was appalled to discover the field his girls played sports on had no outdoor lighting. The girls were so happy to have a program at all that they'd never complained about having to quit practice after sundown. The *boys*, on the other hand, had lighting. When Portantino discovered the girls didn't have the same facilities as the boys, he did something about it.

In many cases, girls don't even think to complain or ask for what the boys have. And maybe the sports department was just as unconscious about the situation. It took a parent intervening on behalf of his daughters because he knew what they deserved: the same respectful treatment given the boys.

After you read this book, if you decide the girls in your school, club or organization need self-defense training, it'll benefit you to know there are frequently hidden concerns or prejudices about what girls need in the realms of physical education, or — even harder to spot — if girls are even *capable* of defending themselves. Some adults have a mistaken belief that if girls learn self-defense, such knowledge will only get them in trouble or seriously injured (or worse), echoing the really bad advice that was routinely handed out in the 70s, "Don't ever fight back… you'll only anger the assailant."

Girls *are* capable and just as potentially athletic or dangerous as any other mammal, and more importantly, they deserve the same attention to physical education as their brothers do.

Stand up like girls, and fight for what you want and deserve!

HAILEY HANDSHAKE

Hailey is a teen who looks like she could be anywhere from 11 to 17. She dresses like other girls her age: short skirts with combat boots, bra strap showing in back. She's fashionable. And when she smiles, she flashes a grill of braces on her teeth like the kid she still is. She attends a private school of mostly affluent students in West Los Angeles, California.

Hailey regularly went to the local mall; it was close enough to walk and all her friends hung out there. They spent most summer days at the mall avoiding the hot, smoggy, Los Angeles weather… and their chores. This day, however, was different. Her Catholic school had the day off, but her public school friends did not. No problem! She decided to spend the day at the mall by herself.

She was strolling along, window-shopping in a mostly

empty mall. She sampled the Chanel No. 5, a scent she loved that reminded her of her grandmother. She felt safe: there were only a few people out shopping, and the security guards all knew her by name.

Hailey had just finished lunch and was walking toward the movie theater to catch the latest summer blockbuster when an older man approached her. He stood in front of her, held out his hand for a shake and said in a smarmy voice, "Hi, I'm Bob."

Hailey took his hand to shake it and enthusiastically said, "Hi Bob. I'm 15."

"Bob" blanched, spun around, and walked away... *very* quickly.

HOW WE SEE IT

Hey, Bob! Where'd you go? Bob? Bob? ... Oh well, we guess Mr. Meet And Greet didn't want to meet Hailey *that* badly.

But that was refreshing, wasn't it? She got straight to the point — quickly. She didn't worry about being rude or hurting his feelings or making him mad or any of the things that often make women hesitate before taking care of themselves. Instead, Hailey was downright friendly while shaking Bob's hand!

Some of you may be aware of the term "jail bait." If you're not, it's a mostly minimizing term for a minor who looks attractive and more mature than her actual years. In most developed countries, a minor is someone who has not reached the age of "majority" or "consent," another way of saying that the person is not considered old enough to do adult things — including driving, voting … and sexual activity.

For some states or countries such as the United Kingdom, that age is 16 although that's on the younger side. In most of America, 21 is the "magic" year that people are considered to be grown up enough to make decisions on their own. To make things even *more* confusing, there are places that let 14 year-olds drive because it makes sense in the more rural states, but that same person can't vote until they're 18. We have to stop now before our heads explode.

Anyway, back to minors. Because minors are not considered adults, other so-called adults who attempt to take advantage of a younger person will get into trouble if they do. There is what's called a "presumption" that an adult knows better than to hit on a younger person, whether that young person is male or female. Of course, we all know there are immature adults of all ages. The rules about sexual encounters are especially strict. If an older person has an amorous relationship with a minor, they can wind up in prison if caught … thus the term *Jail Bait* (wink, wink). This is a somewhat sneaky way to alert a prowling older person that initiating sexual relations with a younger person could land them in jail, just like a big ol' fish. Splash.

Hailey was minding her own business when Bob, for whatever reason, decided to get all friendly and see if he could land a fish himself. But Hailey was too smart to let him catch her.

We really don't know Bob's intentions. They might have been innocent; they might have been "fishy." The great part of this story is that Hailey took it upon herself to meet "threat with threat" at the appropriate level. She didn't over-react, nor did she under-react. She sensed that Bob was someone who needed a boundary set, as he might have been "threatening" an inappropriate relationship. In any event, she brought a threat of her own to the table, and in just a few words let him know that if he pursued her, there could be consequences.

Most of us females have been taught to be polite no matter what, and that can lead to being taken advantage of by predators who know that about us, and are even counting on it. Hailey was polite; at just 15, she still let Bob The Lowlife know that she was a person of consequence.

H is for HISTORY

Historically, women and girls who are warriors are considered either freaks or saints — or in the case of St. Joan, both. Joan of Arc was only a teenaged girl when she was burned at the stake after leading an army into battle. She is really the most famous female warrior throughout history, but hardly alone in her bravery. We are all related, at least historically, to a long line of visionary, brave and intrepid girls and women from all walks of life.

While *Hailey Handshake* may not be an historical figure, she is a hero to us. The ease and grace with which she shut down Bob was downright warrior-like and we want to be just like her when we grow up! Historically, people — especially creepy adults with bad intentions — expect girls to not stand up for themselves. Well, Hailey surprised Bob when she did just that. The veiled threat was eloquently put and the creep had nothing else to do but walk away…and that is the greatest success in our minds.

One of the reasons March was declared Women's History Month by federal decree is that most of us know little about women and girls in history: as warriors, defenders or otherwise. It makes a difference to our contemporaries to see whose shoulders we stand on and to see that we're not alone, especially when we contemplate learning something that's considered to be *far* beyond our proper role as a female: self-defense.

When you learn the basics of self-defense, you join the historical spectrum of women and girls who were expected to be the protectors of hearth and home, especially in times of war when the men and boys were deployed to fight battles

— sometimes in far-away places — often leaving home for years at a time. (Indeed, some of them never returned.) The women defending their homes did not say," Oh dear, Mr. Marauder, you'd better wait until my husband or son gets home!" The "men folk" taught them how to use wits and weapons because it benefited the entire family for the "women folk" to know how to defend their land, valuables, loved ones… and themselves.

One of the least known warrior queens, to Americans anyway, has an iconic statue across from the English Parliament, next to the Thames on the Westminster pier. Her name was **Queen Boadicea**, and the statue depicts her holding a spear and driving a horse-drawn chariot, while protecting her daughters and leading troops into battle against the Romans. Now *that's* feminine multi-tasking! (You can see a photo of the statue here: tinyurl.com/Warrior-Statue). She was fierce and selected as the leader of a tribe in the British Roman empire because she was brilliant and fearless. She was royal of course, and very much her own person because she was culturally allowed to express herself.

Every American student knows the story of Paul Revere and his midnight ride, right? (Even though he was "out-ridden" in every way by Israel Bissell, who never got a poem by Longfellow, probably because of his name. But we digress.) On the other hand, how many people know about an equally great Revolutionary war hero in her own right named Sybil Ludington?

According to columnist Bethanne Kelly Patrick, "Colonial women had the same desire for liberty as the men, but did not have the same opportunities to fight for its gain. Perhaps that is why we sometimes overlook heroes like Sybil Ludington of New York's Putnam County, who in 1777 completed a ride every bit as important as Paul Revere's and every bit as treacherous… all at the age of 16, and on bareback!"

Over the centuries, many women had to cross-dress in order to participate in the defense of their countries, and often won high military honors without anyone knowing their true gender identity. Sadly, we'll never know who many of them were because they hid so effectively by passing as a man. There are too many wartime "women in disguise" to name in this piece, although thanks to an unusual gamble from Disney in the 90s that paid off, most of us have heard of the legendary Chinese female warrior Mulan, who dressed up like a man to save her father's reputation and wound up saving the Emperor.

It's interesting to note that cross-dressing becomes more common place during wartime; men often dress like women to avoid fighting or to cross into enemy territory, while women disguise themselves as men to gain access to the battleground in order to find lost loved ones, or yes, to fight.

An informative, entertaining and eye-opening fictionalized account of an actual historical American woman, who disguised herself as a man to avoid attention as an unmarried women in the post-Civil War United States, is told in the powerful 1993 movie "The Ballad of Little Jo." Josephine, a well-bred society woman, became pregnant by a seducer known to her family who refused to marry her. She had her baby and immediately was forced to leave her comfortable upper-middle class home to avoid the terrible scandal, shame and ridicule of having a child "out of wedlock."

After leaving her newborn child with her sister, she traveled to the "Wild West," where she was treated like dirt for being an unaccompanied female. She finally decided she would be safest, and live a much easier life, if she simply started dressing like a man. And so she did. She eventually became a well-respected citizen of a small mining community, voted (remember that men could vote, but women could not until 1920) and even ran for office. It was only upon her death that the other citizens found out "he" was a "she." During a time when women were considered to be inferior to men by virtue of their sex, and because of religious teachings, "Little Jo's" deception was a slap in the face to the status quo. She not only did well as a man, she was a better man than a majority of the men in the town who had voted for him/her.

Knowing *all* the great people of history, not just famous men, contributes a lot to not only women and girls, but also to men and boys. We learn that we are all part of the human family, and that the human spirit transcends gender.

You can also see how one's self-respect and aspirations can be lifted by knowing about who went before you in history and what they did. It's easier to "keep dreaming big" when you know a veritable avalanche of stories involving female courage and bravery that have been lost or considered "not important." In a way, that's one of the reasons we wrote this book; like the thousands of women and girls throughout history whose stories never got told because they were deemed "inconsequential," we wanted to celebrate the victories of women who successfully did The Impossible And Unthinkable (not really) by defending themselves. And as you are learning about these amazing women and girls, their strength, courage and determination will rub off on you. We are, in effect, attempting to create a *modern* history that can be a part of you.

One of the most satisfying parts of watching our students learn how to defend themselves is to see them join hands across the centuries with the women, teens and girls who have gone before, in a long, unbroken line of strong, dedicated and courageous citizens who happened to be female.

INEZ INTERVENER

Imagine a lovely summer day on one of the old-fashioned wooden piers in Redondo Beach, California — the quintessential Southern California surfer's paradise. The sound of waves, seagulls and frolicking beachgoers wash around you, as the smell of salt air and the aroma of fried seafood waft by. Inez, a young woman in one of our high school classes, was suddenly shaken from her peaceful stroll on the boardwalk with the sound of yelling.

She looked around: to her right she saw a tall, heavy-set white dude in his 40s yelling at a petite Asian woman in her 30s. The woman was a vendor at one of the tourist-type booths common to seaside attractions. As Inez focused her hearing, she could identify anti-immigrant and racial epithets meant to hurt and provoke. The Asian woman was seemingly paralyzed with fear. Then the Asian woman's young son — also small in stature — stepped between the mother and the race-baiting bully.

Inez thought "This can't be good," and decided to intervene.

She walked over, put her hands up, and stood in "ready stance." She used her hands in a placating manner while saying very gently, "No." She continued with a calm yet strong manner and tone saying, "No, no, no" and the harasser finally just backed away.

When he got a good distance away from the mother, son and Inez, the big bigot gave them another verbal volley. The son started to get riled up and Inez calmed him down with, "It's OK, just let him be. He can't hurt you from there. He's leaving. It's OK."

HOW WE SEE IT

We are impressed with Inez! Most people would have just walked on and ignored this unfortunately all-too-common confrontation. In fact, many people walked past that day without so much as a word to the assailant.

Assailant, you ask? But he wasn't attacking her, right? We beg to differ — and we rarely beg for anything that's not covered in chocolate. A verbal assault is just as frightening as a physical attack. Most physical assaults begin with a verbal barrage. This big aggressor was trying to control the mother and her son by showing them how strong and mean he could be. Inez wasn't falling for it.

But everything is a strategy. Dealing with this racist simply required some finesse to keep it from going physical. By getting between the threatening man and the boy, Inez created what we call a "pattern interrupt." He's probably done this kind of thing before and expected a specific response. When Inez stepped in front of him, she threw him off his game and it became too uncomfortable to continue. Aggressors and other cowards will usually run away when the target resists.

Also helpful: our gregarious graduate used the universal symbol for "calm down," starting with her hands in the ready position and slowly lowering them down… up and down, up and down. Looking him square in the eye showed she was not afraid of him, which subconsciously made him afraid of her. Maintaining calm in the midst of chaos is only common for people who deal with fear and adrenaline on a regular basis, so when the "regular folk" are calm like Inez was, it upsets the attacker.

And finally, letting the bully have the last word was also a smart strategy. By not responding, Inez avoided a re-engagement and allowed the guy to think he had won. Of course, to everyone else who witnessed the assault, Inez was hero of the day!

I is for INTUITION

As we've mentioned, our bodies are ingeniously designed to protect themselves, and included in that design is a highly sensitive alarm system routed through our senses, beyond our logical brain. Our senses are "early warning systems" designed to keep us safe. These early warning systems work in conjunction with our other systems for survival. Innate reflexes, intuition, fight-or-flight reactions, and flinch responses — just to name a few — help us quickly make decisions and automatically respond to danger. For example, when something comes flying at your face, by the time you think about stopping it your flinch response has already kicked in and is raising your hands and turning your body away from the danger. Recent brain research has actually proven that the brain sends out signals to act *before* you are conscious of the action itself.

In our opinion, the most important tool we've been given is Intuition. People experience intuition differently. Men will call it a "gut feeling" and women will often say "I just had this feeling…" Your intuition will tell you when something is wrong, and most of the time, your intuition will be right.

Inez Intervener's intuition told her that she would be OK if she intervened on behalf of complete strangers. While it's a personal choice to intervene or not, a significant aspect of "bully" prevention is now focusing on coaching bystanders to get involved, instead of ignoring a scene and walking on.

If we understand intuition, we can hone it and use it to our advantage in many areas of our lives, not just for staying safe. Many of us have experienced the feeling of *just knowing* the decision we are making is right, or meeting someone for the first time and "clicking" with them, getting along with them right away. We believe these feelings also come from our intuition. In the same way, it gives us information that helps us determine if we are in danger; intuition also makes the connections that help us determine if things are right or good.

The Safety Godmothers have a non-scientific way of describing how intuition works: your system takes in all kinds of information through all of its senses and then devises a response. All day long you experience sounds and smells; you touch and taste and see things, many of which you are not consciously aware. Then at night, while you sleep, your brain processes all of the information and files it for retrieval later. That's why you may have crazy dreams, like "why is that dolphin driving a car…?" Your brain is trying to figure out how all the information fits together. Then later, when you encounter a stranger for example, your brain will compare what's in front of you with all of the information it has gathered and give you a sign. Some people feel the hair on the back of their necks stand up, some people get goose bumps — everyone is different — but we all get some kind of sign. And this happens in nanoseconds. Amazing! With all of this creative work going on inside us, we're always surprised when people don't trust their intuition, and talk themselves out of their own experience.

On the same note, someone may approach you to ask a question and you feel relaxed; none of your alarms are going off. That's intuition, too, telling you things are fine.

You may have heard someone say "if my dog likes you, then you are OK with me." In light of new scientific revelations of how dogs interact with people, what's probably going on is that the dog is not making its own intuitive decision; rather, the dog is "reading" its master's eye movements, emotional state and body language, and will react one way or another depending on how the master responds. So we guess it's OK that you trust your dog's intuition, since she or he is simply reading yours. Brilliant!

Students often ask us questions like, "How will I know if the guy asking me for directions means me harm or not? What if he's really just asking for directions, and instead I tell him to take a step back... won't that just make him angry?"

This all boils down to a very simple, yet profound question: "What if I'm wrong?" What if my intuition tells me something and because of that I hurt a person's feelings or anger them?

The first thing we want to say is that you *cannot* turn a normal person into an assailant. If, for example, a man approaches you and asks for directions and your intuition tells you to ask him to take a step back, the way he responds will give you all the information you need at the conscious level. A normal man who means you no harm will probably just apologize and take a step back. A man who means you harm will likely get angry at the request. There is your answer! If he gets annoyed with you for setting a boundary, you need to be prepared to protect yourself.

On another note, if your intuition tells you something is wrong with the situation in front of you, and you respond by getting into ready stance and looking like you are aware and therefore not a good target, he may just walk away — problem solved. You may not know for sure if he actually meant harm, but it doesn't matter, as long as you are safe.

Learning to respect your intuition will serve you well in life.

JULIE JUSTICE

Julie is a dreamer. She is also naive, and — as a newly minted freelance graphic artist — has to frequently travel around the greater Los Angeles area by herself. She had not taken a self-defense class in her high school, even though she had the opportunity. After much prodding from her friends, she finally took our class. At her graduation, she was ferocious! The class changed Julie's life. At the time, she had no idea she would soon have to employ her newly acquired skills about protecting herself from violence.

Julie's boyfriend was anxious for her to move in with him. She'd been indecisive for almost a year. "Enough," he said. For some reason, she wasn't excited about the idea. Finally, against her better instincts, she relented since she felt she needed to get out of her parents' home.

Three months in, Julie decided their living arrangement wasn't working. Her boyfriend was controlling, and had started trying to keep her from seeing family and friends — a classic warning sign for impending domestic abuse. He suggested they get a dog together, which she didn't want; he got one for her anyway as a birthday gift, despite her having previously refused it. Finally, without confronting him directly about his behavior, she told him she was moving out because of finances and would be returning to her family's home.

The boyfriend went to bed and fumed. Finally, in the wee hours, he came into the living room where Julie had been staying that night and freaked out, yelling and screaming and finally throwing an iron at her. Thank goodness the iron did NOT hit her head, but her arm instead. He shoved her up against the wall, backed up and began to "shark her": pacing back and forth in a slow, menacing stride, presumably working out what he was going to do next. Julie shook off her shock and realized, "Hey, a man I thought I loved is assaulting me!" and shifted into defense mode.

She transformed from Julie Ever-Nice to Julie-Justice. She took a "ready" stance and held her hands up to protect her center-line (the area with all the vital organs) and head. She yelled, not screamed, for him to "back off." She'd already rehearsed this in class so she didn't have to figure anything out in the moment. He knocked her down. She knew to keep her legs between herself and her attacker, kicking at his vulnerable targets; she also knew that she was most dangerous there. "On the floor" is a powerful position for a woman whose legs are usually stronger than a man's arms. Think about it: no matter how large the man, his arm and fist are no match for a leg on any size woman who knows how to use it. She pivoted on her butt and kept her kicking leg between her and his fists and kicks. Frustrated, he left the apartment.

She won. She protected herself and got away with no more than a few bruises. She now has a 5-year restraining order against him. She learned, as so many have learned thanks to our classes, that she should always listen to her intuition, that a person who ignores "No" is highly suspect, and that her safety is worth fighting for.

HOW WE SEE IT

We have so much to say about domestic violence that we don't know where to start. For starters, how unjust it is that some women's homes are places of abuse rather than rest and nurturing. The old saying, "A man's home is his castle" ought to apply to women and girls too, but often doesn't. On one hand, we want to be treated with respect. We are conditioned from the time we're little girls to expect the knight in shining armor to come and whisk us away to the happily-ever-after ending. On the other hand, we feel too shy to make reasonable demands to be treated with respect. So, when a man wants us so badly that he becomes possessive, we sometimes confuse that with love. Often, as nurturers, we don't want to ruffle any feathers or hurt people's feelings or believe the ones we love could really hurt us. When our abuser says he's sorry and won't do it again, we want to believe him.

The quest for justice must start with the ones closest to us if they are treating us badly. We need to be our own rescuers and to seek the justice we deserve.

According to DomesticViolenceStatistics.org, as of 2012, on average more than three women *a day* are murdered by their husbands or boyfriends in the United States.

The statistics on domestic violence are so horrible, we have trouble not retching all over our computer as we write about it. For example: the highest rate of death in the workplace for women is murder by a loved one who has followed her to work. Here's another statistic, quoting directly from Gavin de Becker's indispensable *Gift of Fear*:

"…if a full jumbo jet crashed into a mountain killing everyone on board, and if that happened every month, month in and month out, the number killed still wouldn't equal the number of women murdered by their husbands and boyfriends each year." (Chapter 1, pg. 8)

Could we rouse some major indignation here? At this point, you may be asking why women and girls stay in abusive relationships. We don't have a really good answer for you… well, we do, but that would be a whole other book. The point is, we don't really care why; we just want to help them get out of bad situations. The longer the relationship has gone on before the violence begins, the harder it is to get out, especially if children are involved. Mothers are often afraid of making it worse for everyone, or leaving the kids behind. In addition, battered women often don't have their own form of income, so they are literally reliant upon their abusers for their survival — a very sticky situation, indeed.

Luckily, Julie got out right away. How fortunate she had already taken self-defense training *before* the violence began. She knew from the beginning that something was not right. She was reluctant to move in with him from the get-go, but she never expected violence from him. Julie learned that her life was worth fighting for and that she has the right to defend herself against anyone who means her harm. You can bet Julie will never disregard her gut feeling like that again.

Had she allowed him back into her life, he probably would have cried, told her how much he loved her and swore he would never do it again … all lies. You don't abuse people you love; you abuse people you see as your property, with many people abusers starting their physical abuse career with animals. And, like most violent offenders, the domestic abuser will not stop; in fact, the violence will only get worse until he eventually maims or kills his kids, girlfriend or wife.

As harsh as this may sound, there is nothing you can do to help someone like this. Those who abuse others need competent therapy, or at the very least counseling, if they wish to lead a normal life. This is a choice only they can make, and no one else can make it for them. It all really comes down to your choice to either stay in an abusive relationship, or be free of it. Or better yet, to not be in such a relationship in the first place by trusting your intuition.

On the Lowlife Spectrum, we believe domestic abusers should be ranked at the very bottom: right down there with the pedophiles and anyone who uses their social status to abuse others.

J is for JUSTICE

As *Julie Justice* showed us, we need to address the topic of justice in a book about self-defense because the subject often comes up in various ways. A common reaction from prospective students is, "It's not *fair*! Why should *we* have to learn how to defend ourselves? The violent ones should stop being violent!"

It certainly was not "fair" that Julie had to defend herself against someone she thought she loved. It was not "fair" that she wasn't free to speak up for herself or make decisions about her life that were best for her. But she did get justice when she defended herself.

Here's the thing: we agree with those sentiments. It's *not* fair or equitable that people who are (for the most part) peaceful need to prepare for people who are aggressive, whether it's verbal, emotional or physical aggression. Sadly, the planet "Fair" is light-years away from the planet "Reality," and we don't have a starship that can make the journey, which is why we need to deal with reality.

And here's a big dose of it. According to the organization *One In Four USA* — www.oneinfourusa.org

- One in four college women have survived either rape or attempted rape in their lifetime. The US Department of Justice published a study in 2006 of over 4,000 college women. In that survey, 3% of those women had survived rape or attempted rape in just a 7 month academic year. An additional 21% had survived rape or attempted rape at some point in their lives prior to that academic year. When you take those two figures and add them up — the 3 and the 21 — you get 24%, or roughly one in four.

And the rate is slowly but steadily rising.

- In a study by the U.S. Centers for Disease control of 5,000 college students at over 100 colleges, 20% of women answered "yes" to the question "In your lifetime have you been forced to submit to sexual intercourse against your will?" Thus, one in five college women has been raped at some point in her lifetime.

- In a typical academic year, only 3% of college women report surviving rape or attempted rape. This does not include the summer, when many more rapes occur.

- In the year 2000, 246,000 women survived rape and sexual assault. This computes to 28 women every hour.

- A survey of high school students found that one in five had experienced forced sex (rape). Half of these girls told no one about the incident.

- Rape is common worldwide, with relatively similar rates of incidence across countries, with 19% – 28% of college women reporting rape or attempted rape in several countries. In many countries, survivors are treated far worse than in the U.S.

If that wasn't enough, according to the Rape, Abuse & Incest National Network (RAINN), women report abuse at much lower rates than it actually occurs! In their studies, 44% of victims are under the age of 18, and 60% of sexual assaults are not reported to police.

In what we think epitomizes the unjust nature of living within a rape culture, consider this quote: *"Once, in a Cabinet meeting, we had to deal with an outbreak of assaults on women at night. One minister suggested a curfew: women should stay home after dark. I said, 'But it's the men who are attacking the women. If there's to be a curfew, let the men stay home, not the women!'"* — Golda Meir (1898-1978), Prime Minister of Israel from 1969-1974

While men are far more likely to commit violence than women, both genders are capable of it. Speak to any ER personnel, or mental health emergency worker, and they can tell you that women can also be violent.

It's also true that fairness doesn't figure into other matters of safety. It's not fair that people drive drunk or even drive under the influence of being a bully. What we call "road rage" is a form of bullying, in which a car is a deadly weapon.

Just as fear can both serve us and hinder us, so can notions of fairness and justice. If you have a strong feeling that something's not *just*, whether that thing is a personal relationship, at home, or at a school, you've got a golden opportunity for action. That feeling of indignation, or that something is unjust, is a great jumping off point for seeing what actions you might take to bring fairness to the equation. We're going to suggest that nurturing feelings of "unfairness" *without* action is not very productive and may serve to grind us down in the long run.

More good news: Learning how to defend yourself is a positive action and is not rocket science. And people who are aggressors are not geniuses!

So basically, our position is that taking a self-defense class is a way of leveling the playing field, and a way of taking action against a social injustice which not only impacts us personally but culturally.

Sadly, most "ending violence against women" measures or initiatives only address situations *before* violence happens (prevention), or *after* (what to do if you've been assaulted).

The Safety Godmothers are all for prevention and dealing with the aftermath of violence. But we go a step further: we are the mavens of what to do *during* an attack, and are committed to having those "during" tools available to as many people as possible.

Returning to the subject of justice, here's something else to consider: it is extremely unjust that quite a few women and girls *curtail their freedoms* because of fear. Here's an example.

One of our class participants had been violently assaulted ten years prior to taking the course. To deal with the trauma of that attack, she had restricted her world to activities that only occurred during daylight hours. She refused to ever go anywhere after dark, even with other people, and went out only on rare occasions when she couldn't get out of the activity. She was living in a very small world.

After her self-defense training, she was *ecstatic* when she let our former Executive Director, Heidi Hornbacher Cavagna, know that she had gone out to meet girlfriends — at night — for a glass of wine.

Not a big deal for some of us, but for *her*? Huge. And a triumph of personal action that translates into making her life more open, more expansive, more free… and therefore, more just.

On the other side of the justice coin, let's flip the "justice/fairness" balance here for a second and look at what's not fair for men and boys.

Men have an unfair cultural expectation that they *should* know how to protect not only themselves but their loved ones, even if they've never been taught what to do. They are expected to be the ones that step forward when there's danger. Talk about unfair!

In the animal kingdom, both females and males step forward when there's danger or the threat of harm. If they are a prey-type animal, like animals that run in herds, they *all* run. There's no "gendered" reaction to danger for other animals. However, part of the injustice of violence against women and girls is they've been virtually "declawed" and taught to expect that a male will protect them, as they are physically incapable of doing so themselves.

That's where we come in! We are the missing piece. As we've shown, females are utterly capable of defending themselves, but they must be taught how and shown that it is their right to do so. And then, just like males, they will have the tools to decide when and if they will use those tools. Educational injustice happens when we systematically deprive girls and women of defensive tools that are their birthright just by virtue of their sex.

Susan B. Anthony, one of the women who inspired other women to fight for their right to vote, said, "I declare to you that woman must not depend upon the protection of man, but must be taught to protect herself, and there I take my stand." She said that in the late 1800s. We're saying it in the early 21st century, and that's our stand too!

KATIE, KITTY SAVER

Katie and her family live in the hills around Silver Lake, an idyllic neighborhood in Los Angeles that is a mix of urban and rural. The perfume of flowers and citrus trees is a near constant all year round. Like many such neighborhoods in Los Angeles, there is also the possibility of having an encounter with a coyote.

There is a significant coyote population all over Southern California, but especially in the areas with hills and trees. Coyotes generally stay away from populated areas, but as more of their territory is eroded by development, the more they come into residential communities to "grocery shop" for domestic pets, such as smaller puppies and kitties.

Katie was in her living room studying for finals when she heard a neighbor yelling. She went outside and heard her neighbor yell, "Katie, a coyote has your cat!"

Katie didn't stop to talk. She shot off like a bullet and ran down the street after the coyote who then dropped her precious kitty, Tiger.

When we asked her how she had the courage to run after a coyote, she answered, "Easy. After my self-defense class, I realized I had the courage to save myself or others I care about. Tiger is like my child, so I had to at least try. I didn't think about it — I just took action."

HOW WE SEE IT

People are often amazed when a woman of any age does something like chase a coyote that has her cat. But that's because we forget human females are dangerous mammals, too. If you mess with our babies, whatever our age or the species of our babies, you will face our wrath!

But when we had a closer look at this story, what really got us was the reaction of the coyote. It saw a *human* coming after it, not a male or female. The coyote could have clamped down harder on Katie's cat, and continued running like most other wild animals would have. Instead, the coyote saw or felt something that made it change its mind. We wish we could ask the coyote what it was about this situation that turned that particular "un-wily" coyote into a scaredy-cat.

We do know that adrenaline-state training works in all sorts of stressful events, even ones that don't involve a predator or assailant.

Specifically, we know of a woman who was able to save her husband's life when he had a cardiac arrest. She duplicated what she'd learned in class, which was to yell "No! Call 911!" In a twist of circumstances, she was yelling at *herself* instead of at others so she wouldn't freeze, or worse pass out from stress and anxiety.

She kept yelling "Call 911!" until she could get to the phone and actually call 911. The paramedics credited her with saving her husband's life due to her fast action, and she credits her training that gave her the ability to keep yelling and stay present. There was no "self-defense" to speak of; preservation of her husband is more like it. Similarly, Katie used her skills to save her pet.

In a terrifying circumstance, whether it's a medical emergency or the kidnapping of a beloved pet, we know it works to practice safety skills under the type of stress we produce artificially in class. That coyote didn't expect Katie's response. We are pretty sure the intensity emanating from Katie as she chased after her precious Tiger was what scared the coyote. We are certain Katie would have behaved with the same courage if it had been a human assailant attacking her or a loved one… human or feline.

K is for KICK

The Safety Godmothers *love* to kick! Kicking plays a big a role in our system of self-defense. We kick from the ground, we sort of kick standing up (more on that later), and we even teach our kids' class students to kick! We're pretty sure you've heard the phrase, "Get up and fight like a man." Well, one of our favorite phrases is "Get down and fight like a woman!"

What we mean by this is that we teach women to fight from the ground. If a man is going to attempt a forced sexual assault, he will most likely get the woman to the ground; many fights for men end up on the ground as well. For a woman, though, her natural power can really be used on the ground, as a woman is powerful from the waist down while men are primarily powerful from the waist up.

At this point, if you've been following the format of our book, you're probably wondering how we will work "Kick" into the story about Katie saving her cat Tiger. OK, how about this: almost anything we teach about defending yourself from humans can be used with animals, including going for their eyes, or if down on the ground, kicking their head. While kicking wasn't necessary to get Tiger away from the coyote, all of Katie's tools were at her disposal. As it turned out, her voice and indignation was all she needed.

With human defense, a person might be knocked to the ground by the would-be assailant, or may choose to get on the ground first, rather than being at the mercy of the assailant throwing them down. Essentially, what we do is take a frightening prospect for nearly every woman — what if someone tries to rape me — and we demystify it.

Our training is "scenario-based": that means we look at the

actual ways women are attacked, and we teach you to fight your way out of those circumstances. We teach you skills that you will be able to use in any situation so you don't have to think about what you are "supposed" to do; you just defend yourself. Once you see that it's pretty simple to speak up for yourself and to fight for your safety, the mystery is gone and all of the myths about women and violence are cleared up. The biggest myth of all — the one we *love* to bust — is the one that says women cannot defend themselves. We know this is not true! As you've already seen, we have the proof.

Back to kicking: It takes *years* to master powerful, effective standing kicks, especially those delivered while in motion. You've probably seen some of the fancy martial arts-type "spinning" kicks in movies or on TV. They are popular with fight choreographers because they look great on film; in the real world, however, they are impractical. **The Safety Godmothers** believe it's difficult for women to deliver strong, high kicks while standing, because our center of gravity is at our hips. It's not impossible, of course — you can do anything if you set your mind to it — but most people don't want to spend years mastering an art, when what they're really looking for is reliable self-defense.

One of the biggest hurdles we face in our classes is convincing students that they are strong enough to defend themselves. What usually hits home for them is when they actually get on the ground and kick with all their might. Nearly anyone with a little bit of fighting spirit can kick hard enough to stop an attacker in their tracks. We say "nearly" because one of our favorite students has cerebral palsy and she doesn't kick much, but she is meaner than a Honey Badger when she defends herself with rapid-fire eye strikes. Her fingers fly toward an attacker's eyes, which makes any size predator back off! When one of our students finally taps into their full power, it's like a switch is flicked: from that point forward, they hit and kick harder and harder.

We can hear you asking, "What *kind* of kick? How do I kick? *Where* do I kick?" In the previous story of *Julie Justice*, we see that she dropped to the ground and kept her legs between herself and her attacker. The kick we use in our classes is what we call a "side-thrust kick" from the ground. The idea is to keep your legs in between you and your assailant. For a visual overview of this particular kick, IMPACT Bay Area has a great video that shows it in detail; click on tinyurl.com/STKick to see it in action.

The are a few other kicks we teach. One is an Axe kick, which is what you use to "finish" a fight. Another is a knee to the groin (that's the "sort of" kick mentioned in the first paragraph) that can be done both from the ground and standing. Even a light kick to the groin can reduce your attacker to a blubbering pile of tears; a solid kick can often induce *extremely* high pain levels — even vomiting and fainting. Skeptical? Ask any man or boy if such a strike to the groin would hurt, and watch their facial expression when you simply pose the question.

And finally, the kicks we teach in the kids class are snap kicks to the groin and a kick to the shin. The snap kick is done standing and is similar to the knee strike. The shin kick is, of course, a kick to the shin. Recall the pain of running into a coffee table. Ow, right? If you want to drive home a point but don't want to permanently harm someone, a swift kick to the shin will ensure that someone listens to you quite differently. This is also a great "date gone bad" technique if your date isn't listening to your persistent "no, I don't want to go any further…" protests, or "I said stop." Trust us, a swift kick to the shin will get his attention!

For an overview of these various types of kicks, you can go to our YouTube channel at tinyurl.com/IMPACT-LA and check out the posted videos. Seriously, you should watch some video segments first — or have some in-person instruction — before trying to do this on your own. Our main point in talking about kicks is not so much about the techniques involved, but rather to illustrate just how valuable kicking is in the world of self-defense for women and girls.

The wisdom of the phrase "get down and fight like a woman" becomes apparent when you see that a well-placed kick from someone on the ground is powerful, effective and strong. We get a kick out of teaching people just how devastating a ground kick can be. Sorry, we couldn't help ourselves!

LINDA LEAVE NOW

Linda, a self-acknowledged moocher, managed to snag a 5 flight walk-up apartment for her and her boyfriend Kevin to stay in while they were visiting New York City. It was in the Little India part of Queens: not a bad neighborhood as bad neighborhoods go, but definitely not upscale either.

They were coming home from a late night walk. The couple turned down a little side street. Linda was walking briskly ahead of Kevin because it was cold, and she not only wanted to get back to the apartment to warm up, but simply walks faster than he does. A man in a doorway suddenly turned onto the street and was now between Linda and Kevin. It became quickly apparent he was following Linda, who picked up on the "vibe" right away. She stopped to look in a window, but she was really using window shopping as a pretext to get a good look at him in the reflection. She could smell booze from 15 feet away. She moved again. He moved again. She stopped. He stopped.

Finally, she quickly turned around to face him, put her hands up in a "ready stance" and said in an intentionally lowered, soft, yet commanding voice, "Leave now. You do *not* want to mess with me!" He said, "Understood" and scurried away. (Actually Linda used a more, er… *colorful* word for "mess," which was totally appropriate for a New Yorker.)

Kevin, who had watched the whole thing from several yards away, asked, "What did you say?" Linda told him and Kevin said, "He got *that* right."

HOW WE SEE IT

Linda and Kevin were coming home from a late night walk. There's the first mistake: out-of-towners who don't know the neighborhood. They were from Los Angeles, where nobody walks during the day *or* night!

And can we just say, what's all this talk about good neighborhoods vs. bad ones? Where do bad people go to do bad things? In the slums? No! They go to the "nice" neighborhoods! OK, that feels better. Actually, we're kidding: crimes happen anywhere and everywhere. It's a fool who thinks their neighborhood alone will keep them safe.

Linda says the man started following her. How did she know he wasn't taking a late night walk just like her? She knew because she trusted the feeling in her bones which told her something was wrong. She trusted her feelings, and acted on them.

Linda stopped to look at a window — a brilliant tactic. Well, it would have been brilliant if she were looking at the Barney's window rather than the lobby of a tenement building, but whatever... when the man stopped at the same time, then started up again when she did, it could not have been clearer than if he were wearing a sign that read "trouble."

And the smell of booze is always a dead give-away; you should not be able to smell booze on someone 15 feet away from you. If you do, it's a good bet they are smashed. A zonked assailant is good news in some ways. They are generally not in control, especially of their motor skills.

Linda didn't need much convincing that the erstwhile mugger was on her trail. She's a smart gal and just listened to her intuition and read the signs.

What she did next is a classic self-defense avoidance technique: she faced him in ready stance, she looked calm and prepared, and she spoke to him in a deep voice that conveyed the seriousness of the situation, rather than the fear he was expecting.

According to an on-going Bureau of Justice study called the "National Crime Victimization Survey," 3 out of 4 times, if a woman puts up *any* kind of resistance to a sexual assault, the assailant will flee. If she looks confident and alert, he is likely to walk away. He's not looking for a fight, he's looking for an easy target. Linda did a great job of trusting her intuition, and reacting smartly and quickly.

L is for LEADERSHIP

We are not only in the personal safety business, but the courage and leadership business. We can't call ourselves IMPACT Personal Leadership, or IMPACT Personal Courage, although it would be completely truthful to do so. Come for the self-defense, leave with a renewed experience of courage, self-expression and leadership! Pretty great, huh?

In *Linda Leave Now*, it took courage for Linda to lead the potentially dangerous man down the street, keeping an eye on him, knowing he was up to no good. With 8 words, she made it clear to Mr. Up To No Good that he was messing with the wrong person… in our book that is good leadership!

Over the years we have noticed that, time and again, our teaching has "unrelated" or corollary benefits while our students are learning physical self-defense.

What we repeatedly see with our students is that once we practice standing up for ourselves in a stressful situation, we can apply that to many areas of our lives. Here is what may be an odd, but useful example of leadership.

Sharon, one of our students, was in a car accident. She pulled over, as did the man who collided with her. He began to vehemently yell at her in a foreign language. His face was turning purple with rage, and his veins were bulging. Our student had learned how to meet a person's anger by matching their level of volume, and then de-escalating. She put her hands up, stood in ready stance in case his anger moved from verbal to physical violence, and yelled at his level, "Sir! Sir! Sir! Please stop yelling! I won't speak with you until you calm down. When you speak to me more quietly, we can talk." With each of her words, she got quieter. He calmed down and then spoke English. (It's extremely normal for people to use their first language when something traumatic happens.) They peacefully exchanged insurance information and drove away.

Sharon demonstrated leadership in a one-on-one encounter. If she'd cowered, he may have aggressed. She didn't fight with him. She set a firm boundary, made a firm request and stood her ground. If that's not leadership, what is? She led and he followed her explicit instructions on how to relate to her and their car accident.

While the word "leadership" is commonly used in our society, we believe it could use a make-over, because it often excludes ideas of leadership related to being female.

We invite you to reconsider ideas about leadership, and to look at leadership in new ways. What makes us think that being a mother isn't leadership? Why does leadership within a family not "count" as leadership? Or what about leadership in employment or volunteering as a project manager? What makes us think that leaders are simply appointed or elected officials? And more importantly, why do we think of men as leaders or having leadership qualities more than women?

Leadership means *initiating an outcome that wouldn't have happened unless you took action.* Are you afraid of the person you are interning for because she's often in a foul mood? Afraid to ask for different hours? Perhaps the very thing your supervisor is waiting for is your leadership, the very courage it takes to ask for something you need to make your organization work better for you and everyone else. Or, if you're at work and a co-worker or manager is inappropriate, where do you summon the guts to talk to them or possibly report them?

Leadership *is* the willingness to stand for something, even when you're afraid; afraid that you'll sound stupid, make another person angry, or that no one will follow you or you'll be laughed at. Many people who lead understand they are often doing so simply by virtue of being willing to raise their hand when leadership is required. It doesn't mean they are leaders because they know everything. It doesn't mean they are leaders because they have some type of gene or chromosome that makes them that way. They just … went for it.

Leadership is also the ability to generate "urgency," as in: doing *this* right now is more important than doing *that*, and having the guts to state and commit to priorities. When lots of loud, urgent matters collide, it takes leadership to point "that way!" and then get everyone else to follow along. These are all transferable skills that our students learn while setting boundaries in the scenarios we give them for self-defense.

There's nothing magical in leadership. It's the ability to say "Yes" and then follow your own lead. Simply put, leadership is seeing what needs to be done, and then making sure it gets done. Leadership also means you are willing to face the possibility of failure. But mostly, leadership — just like courage — can be contagious, and more accessible through practice. That's what our students experience and that's what we love to provide.

MARY, MODEL THIS!

Mary was in Osaka, Japan, waiting for a train with her friend. Even though it was a hot day, the train station was peaceful and well-run. Mary and her friend were the only Americans in a line with all Japanese women. Four school girls in uniforms were in front of them, four middle-aged women behind them.

An elderly Japanese man approached, obviously drunk and reeking of alcohol. He started berating Mary and her friend in Japanese, presumably for simply being Americans. Mary immediately got into ready stance, put up her hands and said loudly, "Stop. Don't get any closer. Back up!"

He stopped. His face grew livid. He continued to berate her as Mary stayed calm with her hands up, telling him to back up. He did, even though he did not understand English.

He then lunged toward the school girls. All four swiftly looked at the ground and giggled, as most girls their age would do anywhere in such an awkward and threatening situation. But in a country where being an elder demands respect, Japanese younger people are under a strict code to be respectful, no matter what — even if they are being threatened. He started touching them, playing with their hair, pawing them.

Mary finally yelled, "Leave them alone!"

He again lurched toward Mary. She got ready to defend herself, hands still up, knees flexible, breathing deeply as she had been trained in scenarios with a padded mock assailant. Mary forcefully yelled, "No!" He backed off, then reeled toward the girls again.

This time, the lead girl modeled Mary: she held her hands up in the same fashion and said, "No!" The other girls also raised their hands and yelled, "No!" as Mary had done. He stopped, shook his head in disbelief at the four girls now standing in unity against him, and tottered away. Everyone in line, including the middle-aged women, murmured and nodded in approval, then applauded!

HOW WE SEE IT

This story moves us to tears, as the tools used are so simple yet so effective. The story is also a fantastic example of women and girls of all ages being able to learn from one another. It shows that ideas of self-respect and self-protection are infectious, regardless of culture or language.

If Mary had not been there that day, the drunken dirty old man would have probably mauled the younger girls with no consequences. We're sure that *all* of the women present that day learned a valuable lesson and will probably use these tools again.

In the Japanese culture, it is a sign of respect to look down when someone older or in authority speaks to you. Which is fine with us under most circumstances, but this guy did not deserve their show of respect. The girls' giggling is also a common reaction: teen girls all over the world giggle when they are nervous or in an unfamiliar situation. We know it gives the wrong message, but it is what it is; we just have to learn to work with it.

The girls may have giggled and looked down at first, but once they saw what Mary did and how effective it was — even though they also probably did not understand English — they got the gist of what was going on and they went with it. How very brave of them! Even the older women were in agreement that the girls had a very good response to the drunkard. We suspect all the witnesses that day probably had an anecdote to tell at their dinner tables that night.

Even if you do not react at the very beginning of an assault — you were caught by surprise, you were in denial that it was happening, whatever — it's never too late to change your tactic and set a boundary or defend yourself.

We think Mary made a huge IMPACT on that group of young girls that day, and they were probably surprised at how easy it was to stand up to a creepy coward who preys on "helpless women." Too bad he was drunk and probably does not remember anything about what happened that day.

M is for MUSCLE MEMORY

"Muscle Memory" is a common term used to describe how you remember the physical things you do without thinking. To be clear, it is not really information stored in your muscles; rather, it is stored in your "procedural memory." Procedural memory is where we store information on how to do things. The memory is stored through a gradual process and is readily available for access. Using muscle memory does not require conscious effort because it works behind the scenes, connecting both cognitive and motor skills to produce the result you want.

The Safety Godmothers use this system of learning in their self-defense classes: we call it "layering," while scientists call it "procedural learning." The idea is that you learn one segment extremely well before adding the next. For example, when we teach the confrontation sequence — a scenario in which you face the padded assailant while he confronts you verbally — we do it in steps or "layers."

We start by talking about distance and dynamics (from "The 4D's"), and do exercises to practice those concepts. Then we add the heel palm technique; you learn it, drill it and fight it. Next we add the knee strike; you learn it, drill it and fight *that*. Finally, we add it all the layers together and bada-*bing*! You have a confrontation fight with all of the physical elements in place.

Once you've practiced the physical, we then add the verbal component. Again, you learn the concepts, then you drill them, and finally we add the verbal and physical together into a complete confrontation sequence in which you begin to talk your way out of the situation. But, if or when that doesn't work, you will fight the padded assailant to a completed knockout. (In real life, most people would rarely have to go that far, but in IMPACT we always train for "worst-case" situations.)

In the Japanese train station, Mary employed so-called muscle memory because she'd practiced putting her hands up and yelling "No" calmly and firmly enough times that she didn't need to think about it. It's similar to fire drills, where children and adults are walked through the steps of evacuating from an imaginary burning building.

We recommend the book *The Unthinkable: Who Survives When Disaster Strikes* by Amanda Ripley, although we'd like to talk with her about her apparently limited knowledge of women and self-defense. In any event, she points out that on 9/11 the highest survival rate of any company in the Twin Towers belonged to the company whose head of security had the employees practice evacuating the building via safety routes, over and over, despite their resenting him for doing it. During that horrible morning, the employees went on "auto-pilot" and most were able to evacuate the building successfully.

Similarly, we encourage you to, at the very least, practice holding up your hands and yelling "No" in front of a mirror. If the idea of that embarrasses you, good! Embarrassment can mimic an adrenaline freeze and you can use it to measure progress. Once you can yell no in the mirror without embarrassment, you're ready to employ it when you might actually need it.

You've also probably heard the phrase "practice makes per-fect," right? We believe that "practice makes *permanent*." Because practice *doesn't* always result in perfection: if you practice the same mistake over and over, your muscle memory will store that mistake and you will be cursed to repeat it until you make a conscious effort to change it.

In our classes we make corrections to you in the moment, in the middle of the fight, so the correction is stored immediately. Of course, it still takes repetition to create good muscle memory, but you do not have to practice a skill regularly once you have a good enough grasp of the skill so that it is stored in your procedural memory.

For another example, let's take older relatives who probably learned how to ride a bike as children, then stopped riding as they became adults. Unless they have suffered brain damage, chances are — if they jumped on a bike right now — they would be able to ride almost as well as they did when they were kids. Conversely, they likely had a locker at school with a combination lock whose number sequence they had memorized (cognitive learning), but if you asked them today what the combination was, most would not be able to tell you. What's interesting about this example is that *using* the lock is a procedural memory, but the number that opens the lock is *cognitive*. While some of them may be able to open the lock by remembering the numbers, if you give them the *actual lock*, their hands literally will know how to do it even if they don't remember the combination. Similarly, there are phone numbers people can't remember but, if you put them in front of a phone number pad, they will key in the number right away.

Why does procedural memory last longer than cognitive memory? The theory is that once you connect information with a "procedure" or an action, it gets stored in implicit or long-term memory. This is a very unique area of the brain that is easily accessed, just like short-term memory. The more you do the action, the easier it becomes: this is what people mean when they say they do something so often they can "do it in their sleep." In this way, muscles become accustomed to a specific movement. It's like driving a car: you don't have to think about how to stop a car, just that you want the car to stop, and then your body does the action it knows will stop the vehicle.

While you do not have to consciously access muscle memory — it's there when you need it — it is helpful to hone your skills and review them periodically. Even visualizing the motion will help anchor the process. It's no accident that Olympic bobsled and luge participants are often seen in a hypnotic state before going down the mountain. They are literally visualizing every twist and turn of the course in their minds, as they have done over and over again for weeks prior. Visualizing is a way to exercise the brain's own muscle memory!

NANCY SAYS "NO"

Nancy had just graduated from college, while her best friends from college — Brian and Sheryl — recently moved into a new home. What better time for a party? The married couple invited the whole gang over to their new house for a celebration and barbecue, and Nancy couldn't wait to go. As the night wore on, Nancy drank and laughed and played games with the 30 or so people in attendance. Coming out of her "party haze," Nancy noticed that everyone had left; even Sheryl had gone to bed.

Nancy found herself alone with Brian, Sheryl's husband. Normally this would be a non-issue, as they had been the best of friends for 4 years. They had been in classes together, had hung out together as pals many times over; she had no reason to believe this would be anything different.

The two of them were sitting on the couch talking, when Brian suddenly and abruptly grabbed Nancy and tried to kiss her. She laughed it off and tried to push Brian away. Brian persisted. Nancy said "No," yet he acted as if he hadn't even heard her. She was confused — this behavior from him was so foreign to her she couldn't believe it was even happening! She got up and moved to another couch. He followed her. Nancy again asked Brian to stop, and again he persisted, while upping his game by trying to kiss her and "feel her up."

Nancy said things like, "No. What are you doing? We're just friends." And "No, your wife is in the other room." She got up and moved several times, thinking he would stop, that he was simply drunk and would soon notice that what he was doing was wrong. Nothing phased Brian: every time she moved, he followed. She finally sat in a chair and he sat on her lap. He had her pinned down.

Nancy thought, "This is ridiculous! What am I doing? He's too drunk to even understand the words I'm saying." That's when she finally stood up, dumping Brian on his butt, and clearly said "No, Brian, that is enough!" Then she grabbed her purse, ran out of the house, got in her car and drove away.

The next day she went back to the house to pick up various things she had left behind while escaping the sloppy smoocher. Brian was not there and Nancy decided not to say anything to Sheryl. The next time she saw Brian, he acted as if nothing had happened, as if nothing was different between them. When she brought up the party, all Brian had to say was, "That was a fun night, wasn't it?" That was when Nancy realized he either did not remember the end of the night and his attempted assault, or he didn't see it as a problem. She didn't have the words to explain what happened or how she felt. That's when she decided it would be better to step away from the relationship, to have only limited contact with the couple from then on.

HOW WE SEE IT

Although Nancy had not taken any formal self-defense train-ing, we like her story because she demonstrates that the desire to be left alone and safe is innate in *all of us*, regardless of training.

Distance is a very good boundary. There is no reason that anyone needs, or should put up with, unwanted sexual atten-tion from *anyone*. We expect friends to respect "no" without having to repeat it. Nancy displayed the classic reaction we have when people we know and care about behave badly. We don't want to believe it. We laugh uncomfortably, we don't do anything that will damage the person or the relationship if we can help it. What we often don't realize in that moment is, the relationship is *already* damaged forever; it will never be the same.

When **the Safety Godmothers** hear stories like this, we want you to ask yourself, "Why is it OK for *me* to be uncomfortable, but not *him?*" We don't blame Nancy for not speaking up after the fact, telling Sheryl and confronting Brian; she did a good job of just getting herself out of the situation before things got really bad. This is precisely why we teach verbal strategies in our classes, why we teach people to stand up and speak up for themselves, and why we practice role-playing scenarios with real-life situations that involve both strangers and people we know. This is not easy stuff! Saying "no" to someone you care about, and having it ignored, is a blow to the senses — it smacks of complete disrespect and that stings!

We can't determine whether Brian had a black-out from excessive drinking or not. We don't know if he couldn't recall what he did, or if he didn't think it was a big deal, or if he was just thinking "Well, I was drunk, I didn't know what I was doing." We do know there are alcoholics, and just regular people who might have a little too much to drink on occasion, who would never accost people they care about, drunk or sober. Alcohol doesn't turn a well-intentioned person into a rapist; the rapist or assailant is somewhere in there already. Alcohol does not block your ability to hear "No," but too many people think it is an excuse to do so. This is why we want you to speak up as soon as possible if you find yourself in *any* uncomfortable situation.

While we don't necessarily advocate for "avoidance," Nancy did the healthiest thing for herself that she could at the time, and avoided this couple… for good.

N is for THE POWER OF NO

By special guest contributor Gavin de Becker

Possibly the most valuable word in our language has just two letters: N-O. Though the word NO is one of the most potent words we have, it is among the least popular. In part, that's because we grew up associating that word with not getting what we wanted. Most kids hate the word, but as they grow, there is exceptional value from learning to love it. Though perhaps hard to imagine, this single word can play a central role in our safety, particularly for young women of dating age.

Teaching teens about this isn't easy, because they've learned so much about dating from movies and TV shows. A popular Hollywood formula could be called "Boy Wants Girl, Girl Doesn't Want Boy, Boy Persists and Harasses Girl, Boy Gets Girl." Many movies teach young men that if you just stay with it — even if you offend her, even if she says she wants nothing to do with you, even if she's in another relationship, even if you've treated her like trash (and sometimes *because* you've treated her like trash) — you'll get the girl. Young women will benefit their entire life from learning that persistence only proves persistence and does not prove love. The fact that a romantic pursuer is relentless doesn't mean you are special; it just means he is troubled.

Young women (OK, *all* women) will benefit from understanding the following paradox: men are nice when they pursue, women are nice when they reject.

The most troublesome part of this niceness is the counter-productive practice called "letting him down easy." True to what they are taught, when women are rejecting they often say less than they mean. True to what they are taught, men often hear less than what is said. Nowhere is this problem more alarmingly expressed than by the countless parents, siblings, movies, and television shows all telling young men that when she says NO, that's not what she means. Add to this all the young women who were taught to play "hard to get," when they don't actually want to be gotten at all, and the result is that NO can mean many things in our culture! Here's just a small sample:

- Maybe
- Not yet
- Hmm…
- Give me time
- I'm not sure
- Keep trying
- I've found my man!

There are only a few books in which the meaning of NO is always crystal-clear. One is the dictionary. Another one is the book you are currently reading. As you'll see in these pages, NO is a complete sentence. This is not as simple as it may appear. Understand that when a man in our culture says NO, it's usually the end of a discussion, but when a woman says NO, it's the beginning of a negotiation.

* * *

This is **the Safety Godmothers** again, saying "Thanks, Gavin!" We firmly believe that "no" should not be the beginning of a negotiation: it's time for us all to say what we mean, and mean what we say.

Sure, we believe that girls and boys should be nice and polite to their relatives, as well as unrelated adults. However, politeness and the ability to say "no" are not mutually exclusive. Kids and adults need to be able to say "no" and *mean it* without being humiliated or scolded into putting up with touch they don't want, regardless of the good intentions from Aunt Sylvia, the over-enthusiastic coach, or over-attentive clergy member.

"No" is music to **The Safety Godmothers'** ears, even when we don't always like being told it ourselves!

OLIVIA, OH NO YOU DON'T

Olivia was 14 years old, and had taken a kids self-defense class when she was 11. One day in the late afternoon, Olivia was hanging out in the park with her friends after school when an older boy, Jason, came up to her and put his arm around her shoulder. As is often the case regarding unwanted attention — ranging from bullying or harassment to outright physical and sexual assault — Olivia had to deal with someone she was familiar with. Yes, it's true: around 80-90% of all assaults to women and girls are done by someone they already know.

Olivia knew all about teenage boys; her mom had read books to her, and they talked about anything and everything. Olivia also knew Jason: he was 17 and in high school. Worse, she knew how arrogant he could be, how he considered himself to be a "tough guy," how he thought he was God's Gift to Women. Olivia didn't want this particular boy touching her… it felt disgusting.

She remembered what to do from her self-defense class. She also knew she had to do something to stop him right away, or it would get harder and harder to set a boundary. Resolved, Olivia reached up, took Jason's hand off her shoulder, and handed it back to him. She looked him directly in the eyes and politely said, "Please take your arm away." He laughed and did it again. Olivia repeated exactly what she'd done, except this time with a little more *oomph*, a little more seriousness. Again, Jason disregarded her boundary with a chuckle, and this time put his arm around her waist.

That was it for Olivia. She reached out with her right arm and swiftly pulled it back toward Jason, effectively delivering an elbow strike right to the center of Jason's solar plexus, *hard*, doubling him over and knocking the wind out of him. (The solar plexus is above your belly button and just below and between where your ribs meet. It hurts a lot to get hit there.) She looked down at the pathetic heap that used to be Mr. Tough Guy and said, "Now I'm supposed to knee you in the nuts, but if you leave, I won't do it."

Jason turned and high-tailed it out of the park. Just as she had learned in her class, Olivia went home and told her mother what had happened. Her mom congratulated her and told her she was proud! Then Olivia's mother called Jason's mom and made sure she understood that it was not OK for Jason to touch her daughter or any other girl who didn't want to be touched!

HOW WE SEE IT

Brava, Olivia, Brava! This story has all the elements we love: resolve, boundary-setting, muscle memory and then, appropriate action when those boundaries are ignored or violated as soon as there is an opening! What we're particularly pleased with is that Olivia's training when she was 11 served her well at 14. Three years later, her training kicked in — or, in this instance, elbowed in — and was right there at her elbow tip when she needed it. Also, the beauty of an elbow strike to the solar plexus is that it merely knocks the wind out of someone; it doesn't send them to the hospital. It's related to the shin kick (see *K is for KICKS*) insofar as a shin kick hurts like heck but doesn't cause permanent damage. Elbows to the solar plexus and shin kicks are good for making a point, physically, without causing lasting, permanent harm. In Jason's case, it most *assuredly* got his attention!

One thing we've seen is that little boys are often given permission by their families to set boundaries, but not so much for girls. It's not difficult to remember relatives almost boasting that little Johnny had gotten too big to kiss and hug:

"Why, he just told me to stop hugging him," complains the affronted relative, to which the parent often responds, "He's at that age now. You know, he's growing up."

While it may hurt a bit for the relative to hear that Johnny doesn't want their affection, they will most likely let his boundary stand for what it is: don't touch me unless I say it's OK. In the same situation, however, girls are often told the relative "means well" and urged to be nice, not hurt their feelings, and just put up with the hugging.

We need to teach our girls that it's OK for *them* to assert jurisdiction over their own bodies, just like the boys. After all, if a little girl can't set a boundary with a family member, how the heck is she going to set a boundary later in life with a date, stranger, co-worker or boss. Remember that childhood is the closest any of us ever get to having a rehearsal for real life.

For the most part, we as a culture often give girls a very big unintentional lesson: when we shame them into letting a relative kiss them, pinch their cheeks or hug them, we are telling them that what they want doesn't matter; that the feelings of the relative are more important than her feelings. We inadvertently allow girls to be considered inconsequential if people disrespect their boundaries.

A child's life is just as real to them as our lives as teens or adults. As children, we're bullied, harassed, and challenged with power plays. It behooves us all to give younger kids support in how to negotiate the often difficult waters of being in school or on a playground. Not only will that training serve them later on as adults, it'll even help them during their high school years.

Your **Safety Godmothers** believe it's important to practice, in age appropriate ways, how to have someone STOP doing whatever it is that bothers a child. We value their intuition. We tell them that if something doesn't feel right, that it might not be, and to tell an adult or an older sibling about it. If that person they tell doesn't listen, keep telling until someone *does* listen.

We believe kids should learn that they have jurisdiction over their own bodies. That no one gets to touch them without their permission, including peers. They should learn verbal skills, and then — as a last resort — physical skills that allow them to escape to safety.

Olivia did her best and was indeed very polite with Jason. He disregarded her wishes, and then her demand, to his own detriment. Bottom line: Olivia learned she could deliver consequences to someone who threatened her... someone she already knew. Pow! Right in the solar plexus.

O is for OPENINGS

Are you surprised to see the word "openings" in connection with self-defense and personal safety issues? We don't mean the openings of shows or shops. We mean openings in the sense of opportunities for action.

With the previous story, Olivia had an acquaintance scenario: she knew her opening for action (his solar plexus) was behind her, and she didn't try to elbow an area that was out of range. She knew that if she threw her elbow back, it would connect with her target — POW! His wind was knocked out of him, into the next block.

Stranger rapes are far more infrequent than rapes where the target knows the assailant, but what can be more terrifying than the idea of waking up with a rapist pinning you to the bed in the middle of the night? We have very few images in the media — whether in movies, TV or news stories — where women *successfully* fight back during an attempted or completed rape. Even anecdotally, we rarely speak about rapes or rape attempts.

In our classes, we teach openings by using simulated rape attempts, and we call those scenarios "reversals" because we practice "reversing" the power. While it looks to most people like there's no way to even fight back, we teach our students how to actively search and seek out an opportunity to act, then take charge of reversing the power and successfully resisting a rape attempt.

Our class teaches the student to breathe and take stock, which means… searching for openings. Is his full weight on me? (If it is, there's an opening for me to roll like a log and throw him off.) Did he remove his hands so that he could pull down his zipper? (If so, there's an opening for me to go for his eyes and get my legs between me and him and yell with all my might.)

With familiars or acquaintances ("Oh, yeah, this is the guy who works at the student store") all the way to close personal or family friends, denial is apt to be a *big* factor. "I can't believe this... He wouldn't want to hurt me... Oh, he's just playing..."

Here's an example:

You are hanging out with your guy friend watching a movie. He starts wrestling around with you and tickling. At first it's OK, even mildly funny... but soon it becomes uncomfortable and even scary for you.

You say, "Stop. This isn't fun anymore."

He says, "Sure it is!" and keeps on tickling.

You say, "Stop it. I mean it."

He says, "What's wrong with you? I'm just playing around."

Suddenly, he's thrown you to the ground and is sitting on your chest, pinning your arms to the ground — just like your big brother used to do, only you weren't scared of your brother. Your instincts are telling you this is not fun, something bad is coming. Remember *you* get to decide what's fun for you; fun is when the enjoyment is shared, not when it's at your expense. At this point, ask yourself "Where's my opening?"

Now, here is where things get sticky for us Safety Godmothers; if you two are really just playing around like "guy friends," then what another guy would do is try to wrestle himself to the top, to be the one delivering the noogies instead of receiving them. But as girls, we're generally not taught to play that way — and we often don't think we are strong enough to roughhouse, or we think we would be hurting him instead of playing with him and often stop ourselves from doing so. We've made this analogy before, but if we look at animals in nature both male and female animals practice stalking, hunting and killing with one another from the time they are babies. There's no distinction between male and female when it comes to the survival skills they "rehearse" in play.

So if this is truly an issue of just playing around, you have to set some rules. For example, you both know and agree that when the other person says "enough," or whatever the agreed upon word, both of you stop. If your friend is not able to follow these simple guidelines, then you have just gained some very important information about that person.

Back to the example, and the topic at hand: "Where's my opening?"

Take a deep breath. Stop fighting him and totally relax your limbs; he thinks you are giving up and he loosens his hold on you. You are then able to pull your hand free and go for an eye-jab; you don't even have to connect, because he'll automatically flinch before he'll let you get that close to his eyes. You can then toss him off of you, and start screaming your head off for your mother who is upstairs. You just created an opening!

An empowering aspect of our classes is that all of the students line up as each woman or girl goes out onto the mat for her fight with the padded assailant. The line watches, cheers and calls out openings. By seeing the openings for others, the information gets recorded in the brain of each student, whether they are actually fighting or not.

We are continually told that once our graduates have seen as many fights as they've seen within our class, they are unable to watch movies in the same way again. They see openings, and have to hold themselves back in movie theaters from yelling, "Eyes! Groin!"

There is one more thing about openings. We also train you to avoid providing openings for criminals. When you are aware of your surroundings — which involves being proactive, like not texting while you are walking — you are denying an opening for an assault. However, do not hear that like it's your fault if you're ever assaulted. It is *always* the assailant who is the guilty party. You are not responsible for making someone assault you, even if you're behaving in ways we'd recommend that you not: drinking beverages given to you by others that may contain a date rape drug, wearing ultra-revealing clothing, etc.

The topic of "Openings" really boils down to awareness combined with action. As in, figuring out "what is my opening here?" and then, taking it.

PATTY PETITE AND POWERFUL

Patty stands tall at 4′ 11″ (and ¼, she likes to add), but while her size may be petite, there's nothing small about her determination and skills in staying safe. Patty has always been a spitfire, constantly involved in one project or another or helping out friends in need. This day was no different.

Patty frequently volunteered to help people and organizations in her Southern California desert town. Today, she was dropping off supplies for an upcoming dance and holiday event. There was no one else around and, as the hall is pretty much the only building on the block, there should have been no one else there unless they were helping to set up for the big party. She was walking toward the door with her hands full of boxes and bags — you could hardly see her behind the pile she was carrying —

when from out of nowhere a man walks up to her and says, "Hi there, let me help you with that." Let's call him Scary Scotty.

The hair on the back of her neck stood up; she knew something was amiss. Patty did not argue with what Mother Nature was telling her, which was "something is not right here." She calmly put down all the items in her hands, faced Scary Scotty in ready stance and said, "Stop right there. Don't come any closer." He said, "Geez lady, relax. I'm interested in renting the hall and want to come in and talk to you about it."

On the surface it sounded logical, but Patty knew better. She responded, while not dropping her stance and not letting him talk her out of what she felt, "I can't help you. Call the number on the sign."

Scary Scotty persisted. "Aw, come on, don't be a bitch. Just let me come in and see the place. I'll just look at it and leave, I promise."

Patty remained steady, as she now knew he meant trouble. She was not going to give an inch, or even ¼ of an inch. They stood staring at one another for a few beats. "He is testing my resolve," she thought. She had won stare-downs with some formidable Sicilian grandmothers, so she knew she could stand up to this guy.

Sure enough, the erstwhile thug backed down. As he walked away, she picked up her stuff and without turning her back to the weasel, went into the hall and locked the door.

HOW WE SEE IT

Patty did everything right. Rather than talking herself out of her intuition, she listened to it! We'd like you to — as an experiment — see if you can force the hairs on the back of your neck to stand up. Go ahead. Try to will them to stand. They won't, right? They won't even sit up a little bit on command. So, when the hairs stand up on the back of your neck, or you get goose bumps for no logical reason, you are responding to something that mammals have as a gift — a warning that something is not right, and that something may be dangerous. Patty was not worried. She felt fear and responded to it because she knew her body was telling her something, even if she didn't know what exactly the danger was.

Scary Scotty tried a few tactics: he told her to relax, after surprising her. A person of goodwill would understand that she was startled. He disregarded her desires. A straightforward person would understand and take her directions without arguing by simply writing the phone number down. He gave an unsolicited promise to leave as soon as he had gotten inside. Generally, people don't make promises to leave unless they're covering up an opposite intention.

This is all 20/20 hindsight, right? Here's the main point: we are *really tired* of hearing people say — after becoming a target of a crime — "I don't know how or why, but I *knew* there was something wrong… yet I ignored my instincts. I should have listened to myself."

Patty listened. You can too.

P is for PRIVACY AND CONTROL

By special guest contributor Gavin de Becker

Before Mr. de Becker gets into the juicy subject of Privacy and Control, the Safety Godmothers want you to read his account of what happened on a flight from Chicago to Los Angeles after being a guest on Oprah, *that illustrates a possibly dangerous encounter… except the would-be assailant was unsuccessful in gaining either privacy or control.*

Gavin writes:

I was seated next to a teenage girl who was traveling alone. A man in his 40s, who'd been watching her from across the aisle, took off the headphones he was wearing and cheerfully said to her, "These things just don't get loud enough for me!" He then put his hand out toward her and said, "I'm Billy." Though it may not be immediately apparent, his statement was actually a question, and the young girl responded with exactly the information Billy hoped for: she told him her full name. Then she put out her hand, which he held a little too long. In the conversation that ensued, he didn't directly ask for any information, but he certainly got lots of it.

He said, "I hate landing in a city and not knowing if anybody is meeting me." The girl answered this "question" by saying that she didn't know how she was getting from the airport to the house where she was staying. Billy asked another "question": "Friends can really let you down sometimes." The young girl responded by explaining, "The people I'm staying with [thus, not family] are expecting me on a later flight."

Billy said, "I love the independence of arriving in a city when nobody knows I'm coming." This was the virtual opposite of what he'd said a moment before about hating to arrive and not be met. He added, "But you're probably not that independent." She quickly volunteered that she'd been traveling on her own since she was thirteen.

"You sound like a woman I know from Europe, more like a woman than a teenager," he said as he handed her his drink (Scotch), which the flight attendant had just served him. "You sound like you play by your own rules." I hoped she would decline to take the drink, and she did at first, but he persisted, "Come on, you can do whatever you want," and she took a sip of his drink.

I looked over at Billy, looked at his muscular build, at the old tattoo showing on the top of his wrist, at his cheap jewelry. I noted that he was drinking alcohol on this morning flight and had no carry-on bag. I looked at his new cowboy boots, new denim pants and leather jacket. I knew he'd recently been in jail. He responded to my knowing look assertively, "How you doin' this morning, pal? Gettin' out of Chicago?" I nodded.

As Billy got up to go to the bathroom, he put one more piece of bait in his trap: leaning close to the girl, he gave a slow smile and said, "Your eyes are awesome."

In a period of just a few minutes, I had watched Billy use various "negotiation tactics," including: pretending they were both in a similar situation (both had nobody meeting them), too many details (the headphones and the woman he knows from Europe), and charm (the compliment about the girl's eyes). I had also seen him discount the girl's "no" when she declined the drink.

As Billy walked away down the aisle, I asked the girl if I could talk to her for a moment, and she hesitantly said yes. It speaks to the power of predatory strategies that she was glad to talk to Billy but a bit wary of the passenger (me) who asked permission to speak with her. "He is going to offer you a ride from the airport,"

I told her, "and he's not a good guy."

I saw Billy again at baggage claim as he approached the girl. Though I couldn't hear them, the conversation was obvious. She was shaking her head and saying no, and he wasn't accepting it. She held firm, and he finally walked off after giving her an angry gesture… definitely not the "nice" guy he'd been until then.

Privacy and Control

The man who will attempt to molest a teenage girl needs an environment in which that's possible. He needs to get her to a place where there is nobody nearby who will hear her if she resists loudly or calls for help. His other option is to get her in a frame of mind where she doesn't resist loudly or call for help. Accordingly, there are times and places where wariness is called for, i.e., times of vulnerability. And there are times and places where wariness is wasted, i.e., times when teenage girls are not vulnerable. Dangerous men are only dangerous if they can get you somewhere. They are rarely dangerous on the dance floor, in the restaurant, in the crowded mall. That may be where they meet you, but it's not where they'd try to hurt you.

Do such men actually plot their opportunities? Often, they do, but there is also a type of sexual offender who is on autopilot, operating out of a second nature, an intuitive skill at knowing how to gain control. The good news is that just as he knows when a given environment serves his plans, so can his target intuitively and automatically observe, "I am at a disadvantage here." Since much of what I've said about the nature of men is anything but PC — as in politically correct — I'll borrow the acronym from that tired phrase to characterize the contexts in which young women (and women in general) can recognize their disadvantage: PC will now stand for *Privacy and Control.*

If a man who intends sexual assault or rape has Privacy and Control, he can victimize someone. If he does not have PC, he is not dangerous, period. Accordingly, just the presence of these two features in a situation can trigger a young woman's heightened awareness and readiness. The presence of Privacy does not mean a man is sinister, but it does mean a girl is vulnerable. At that point, she'll benefit from carefully evaluating how the man got Privacy: was it by circumstance or by his design?

Privacy is defined here as isolation or concealment. A private place is one in which there is little or no chance that a third party will suddenly show up, a place that is out of range of the hearing of people who could assist the young woman. Cars, hotel rooms, apartments, houses, closed businesses, wilderness areas, the auditorium after hours, back corridors at work, a remote parking area — these all can afford Privacy.

The word Control defines a relationship between two people; in this case, between a victimizer and his target. Control exists when one person is persuaded or compelled to be directed by the other.

Control can exist when a young woman feels persuaded to do what a man wants because she fears being injured if she resists, or because she doesn't want to hurt his feelings, or because she doesn't want him to hurt her reputation, or because she wants to avoid rejection.

Don't think of persuasion as something someone does to us; persuasion is an internal process, not an external one. We per-suade ourselves. A predator merely manipulates how things seem to us. Whatever the method, persuasion requires the participation of the target, and human beings are the creatures who most cooperate with their predators. By contrast, the lion has a more difficult predatory challenge than does the man who would rape a teenager. The lion, after all, must walk around in a lion suit; he is burdened by the obviousness of the very assets that give him power (claws, teeth, muscle). Hunting would be easy if the lion could look like a timid kitten when it served him. He can't... but a man can.

Some men with sinister intent seek control through physical power. Because the target's resistance might be noisy, the power-predator requires more privacy. He cannot retreat easily because there comes a point where there is no ambiguity about his intent. He commits to likely consequences in ways that most persuasion-predators do not. The power-predator needs more privacy, more space, more time, more recklessness, and more luck in order to get what he wants. Thus, the power-predator is more rare than the persuasion-predator, but also more likely to do serious injury.

The persuasion-predator gets a target to cooperate and is thus granted much more flexibility when it comes to privacy. This man can use a room in the girl's home, even if family members are somewhere in the house. For him, Privacy is adequately afforded by a room at work that people don't frequent, even if the business is open. For him, a few empty seats in a theater can offer enough concealment to sexually abuse a teenager. Accordingly, the teenage girl who can be easily persuaded appeals to a far wider group of predators and is more likely to be sexually assaulted than a teenage girl who cannot be easily persuaded.

Of course, teenage girls will often be in private environments with men who have no sinister intent whatsoever. The driving instructor who takes your teenage daughter all over town is granted some PC opportunities, but if he is a good man, no problem. Still, it's appropriate for a teenage girl to recognize the P in PC is in play, if several turns take them to some remote area.

Ideally, if this occurs, she'd be more alert for the introduction of Control.

Right when a man begins to introduce the P or the C is the defining moment when one can determine — and virtually choose — whether to be a target or a victim. A girl can say, as the driving instructor's directions take them out of populated areas: "I'd be more comfortable staying in the city," or "Please stay in familiar areas." If the man has sinister intent, this girl has just asserted in the clearest language that she will not be easily persuaded, thus his options for gaining control are limited to force or fear, and that requirement will exclude the overwhelming majority of predators.

PC is easy to memorize and recall, because these concepts are already embedded into our consciousness. When someone acts in a way that alarms you, you instantly and automatically evaluate PC whether you're aware of it or not. You intuitively evaluate whether anyone might hear a call for help, or whether someone might come along, measuring what degree of control the predator might have over you. The key — the trick if you will — is to recognize PC issues *before* someone alarms you, even in the absence of obvious sinister intent on the man's part. The impala who finds itself alone with the lion doesn't wait to see how the carnivore will behave; it constantly evaluates its options and resources until the danger is past.

Does this mean a teenage girl must be in a constant state of alertness whenever she is in the presence of men? Absolutely not. This is about being alone with a man in a situation in which she is vulnerable. And then, a recognition of PC might be no more than a passing thought that opens the girl to her intuition about this man. If she feels at ease with her boss at the restaurant, even though there are no customers around, fine. But being cognizant of PC means she'll sooner recognize the slightest inappropriate comment or unusual behavior, like locking the front door before closing time.

Teenage girls: *memorize Privacy and Control*, and when someone has these advantages, be open to signals of that person's intent. That's all I'm asking: not to fear every man, just an acceptance of reality.

Note that I've been using the word target rather than the word victim. That's because being a target need not automatically make one a victim. In fact, it's nearly impossible for a teenage girl to avoid being a target at some point, but it is very possible to avoid becoming a victim. The best way to do that is by recognizing PC at the earliest possible moment, and if things feel uncomfortable (even if it is just the vulnerability itself that feels uncomfortable), taking steps to change the situation.

* * *

This is **The Safety Godmothers** again. We are *deeply* grateful to Gavin de Becker for his intellect and commitment to everyone's safety.

QUINN QUIT IT!

A few years ago, Quinn worked as a summer tour guide at a National Historic Site. She was 17 years old and had been paired with Penny, an obnoxious co-worker a couple of years older. Penny was über obnoxious! For example, she'd hide and jump out at Quinn, then poke and tickle her. Penny's actions weren't exactly mean, but they were annoying and intrusive. Worse, she did not respect Quinn's subtle attempts to get Penny to stop messing around with her.

One day, there were fewer tourist buses than usual, and the constant flow of tourists had ebbed to a mere trickle compared to the floods that were normal. Penny thought this was the perfect opportunity to "up her game." She approached Quinn with both hands shaking and held high, directed toward

Quinn's face and upper body, all the while making weird, haunted horror movie sounds. "Wooo-ooo," she warbled in a tremulous voice, and followed that with unearthly moaning sounds, ending with a sudden and loud "Boo!" in Quinn's face. Penny was trying to be entertaining, but was spooky in ways she didn't intend... like *insane* spooky. Not funny.

Quinn kept retreating from Penny's "horror show" until she could go no further, having backed into one of the monument's classic granite façades. Literally up against the wall, Quinn took the eraser end of the pencil she held and placed it at Penny's throat, at the notch right above her sternum. Although Quinn's heart was beating wildly with all the adrenaline coursing through her system, she remembers managing to say something semi-humorous to diffuse the tension of the moment, like "Back off! Quit bugging me! Do you get my eraser or do I have to make a sharper point? *Back off!*" Penny backed away, mumbling, "I'm sorry. Geez, you don't have to be so crabby" or some other lame excuse that deflected her own responsibility. Penny didn't bug Quinn again after that. Yes, Penny got the point, even if it was only a rubber one.

HOW WE SEE IT

Bullying. It's a bit of a misnomer, because bullying is used to describe a wide spectrum of behaviors ranging from relatively harmless teasing to actual assaults, and everything in between. In this case, there is aggressive behavior that doesn't have harm as an intended outcome, except that the behavior is intrusive or dominating regardless of intent.

A good example of benign aggression: a young Labrador retriever jumps, plays, and maybe drools. The Lab puppy doesn't know her own strength and if untrained, can hurt someone by simply knocking them over or jumping on them. The drool? Well, it's yucky but not violent. Does the puppy intend to be hurtful or sloppy on purpose? No. But one dog's — or person's — playful behavior can be another's annoyance or even cause harm.

There are many types of bullies, to be sure — consider that bullying can sometimes be like bluffing in a card game. The bully is unsure of him or herself and has low self-confidence and self-esteem. He or she blows up some type of action to bigger than life and feels better by imposing themselves on other people. Call the bully's bluff and you get to see the real person: the clueless and often broken person inside. Most bullies or predators will not stop if the intended victim merely ignores them. There's got to be some kind of counter "bluff" or resistance to stop them.

That's what Quinn did. While this may not seem like a bullying situation to you, we are certain it was. Bullying is often in the eyes of the bullied. A co-worker may have been trying to be funny, but when the action stops being funny yet continues, it becomes assaultive. When someone asks you to stop, or gives you all the physical signs of "stop" and you don't, you are bullying, period.

Quinn had several years of martial arts experience under her belt, so to speak. She took a standard technique (a strike to the throat) and toned it way down to suit the actual threat. Now that Quinn is older and wiser, she thinks Penny was possibly lonesome and wanted to be friends, or maybe even had a crush. Nonetheless, Quinn had every right to stop Penny's constant teasing and taunting in the workplace. And the same would have been true had Penny been bothering her at school or anywhere else.

We love that Quinn used a simple tactic to show the bully she was not intimidated. We *really* love that the bully was afraid of an eraser... she got the point, and thankfully she responded to the blunt end.

Q is for QUESTIONS

We've all heard the saying, "There are no dumb questions." While we agree with that in most ways, we are here to say there are questions that can end up scaring you and undermining what you're learning. In our classes, we call them "what if…" questions. There are a few categories of "what if…" questions which warrant a closer look.

When Quinn set a boundary with Penny, she didn't freak herself out with "What if I get in trouble for setting a boundary with this pest?" She did it, and there were no consequences other than the intended outcome; Penny stopped pestering her.

Worst Case Scenario "what if…"

Student A raises her hand and says, "What if you're caught in the crossfire between two warring armies and a tank is bearing down on your girl scout troop?" Our answer? You are S.O.L! But so would a man or boy in the same situation. Don't know what S.O.L. stands for? It's **S****t **O**ut of Luck.

While we are exaggerating with the example, we do have students frequently posing questions in the "ain't-gonna-happen" realm, and we simply say, "That's not likely to happen" and leave it at that. But these scenarios are the stuff of nightmares and really come from a place that's arguing with the effectiveness of what we train people to do. Here is the raw, unvarnished truth: *our training is not designed to handle every situation that's dangerous.* We also can't think of one example of any other form of training or safety device that works 100% every time. And no, *nothing* we teach will work EVERY time under EVERY circumstance. One's imagination can always come up with a hypothetical "what if…" that will invalidate our training.

Never Thought It Was Possible "what if…"

If you grew up with brothers or male cousins, you would *never* ask a question like "What if kicking him in the crotch doesn't work?" as you know that particular "what if…" question is ridiculous! Yet, we often hear students ask it. If you ask that question in a room with men present, they'll cross their eyes and reflexively cover their crotches. Trust us on this one. A more pertinent question would be: "What if I kick for his crotch and he's expecting it and dodges it?" Indeed, if you kick and your foot or knee connects with the front of his pants, it'll hurt — but not as much as when you actually connect with his scrotum. His scrotal sac has so many nerve endings it's a veritable on-off switch; one second the guy thinks "I'm OK," and the next second it's "I'm on the ground retching and experiencing excruciating pain that makes me want to curl up and die."

We definitely coach our students to go for the eyes, the upper "balls" if you will, and once the assailant uses his hands to protect his eyes, go for the lower set of balls. Almost every male has felt what it feels like to get hit really hard there, and they don't need any convincing that a square strike to the groin will do the trick.

The Logical Further Steps "what if…"

We are privy to the great experience of seeing "light bulbs" go off in our students' heads. We are frequently the first providers of personal safety ideas and actions. Because what we do is so simple and so natural, people start thinking ahead and anticipating what will be down the line and begin asking logical "what if…" questions. Examples: "What if you are on the ground, you're preparing a kick and he grabs one of your legs?" If we're far enough along, we show them. Simple — switch to the other side and use your *other* leg! If it's a bit premature, we say, "That's a 'what if…' question and we'll answer it later." There's a tendency to want to jump ahead, especially when you're enjoying what you are learning.

We specifically teach one layer at a time. The analogy to swimming is very useful. When you learned to swim, you didn't go into the deep end first. You first learned to tread water in the shallow end, so that — if you are ever in the deep end with nothing else to use — you can always use the simplest technique in water safety: treading water. Similarly, we have moves that are simple and taught before more difficult moves, but you need to understand and apply them before you move on to the more difficult strikes and kicks. The "what if…" questions, the logical ones, will usually happen in the earlier stages of class.

The upshot is to catch yourself with "what if…" and to foster patience along with your curiosity.

RHONDA RESPONSIBLE

As a young woman, Rhonda had come to Hollywood with the goal of being Queen of All Media. Soon after embarking on her career, she earned herself a coveted intern position as a production assistant for a talk show. Part of her work consisted of going with her segment producer and the video crews to the streets of Los Angeles for so-called "person on the street" interviews. One fine spring day, when the orange blossoms around Southern California were in bloom and spreading their scent all over the area, Rhonda and her crew was in Hollywood asking passersby about their opinions on the Olympics. They'd staked out a place near Graumann's Chinese Theater on Hollywood Boulevard to get a nice cross-section of tourists. As expected, once the video cameras and crew appeared, so did a crowd.

At mid-morning, a young man in the crowd began to harass the production. Part of Rhonda's job description included crowd control, and no matter how much Rhonda talked to him and asked him to go away, the harasser would intentionally run through the shot. Or he'd yell obscenities. Or he'd make "devil" fingers behind the interviewee's head. He was bold, obnoxious... and becoming an expensive problem by ruining shot, after shot, after shot. Rhonda decided she had to get creative to save the day.

She'd taken a self-defense course at her school and recognized that she had adrenaline coursing through her veins, which she knew she could manage. She didn't feel particularly fearful for her physical safety, but she was concerned for her job as well as the success of her crew. They needed to accomplish a certain number of interviews before going back to the studio.

She calmed down, then went directly over to Mr. Camera Hog. She took him aside and whispered, "You know, you've got a great look! If you'll go get a picture of yourself, I might be able to get you on camera. I can suggest it to my producer." He said, "Really?" Rhonda said, "Absolutely!" He ran off and said, "I'll be right back." They moved the crew, and finished the shoot.

HOW WE SEE IT

Rhonda handled the hambone perfectly. This guy had to be a narcissist — all he wanted was to get on TV, never mind the inconvenience and trouble he was causing for Rhonda and her job. He was probably clueless about the time and money he was wasting. As long as he got his mug on the tube, he was happy.

Other forms of cajoling did not work on the guy, nor did reasoning or threats; Rhonda's tactic to play on his self-absorption was perfect. But c'mon, did he really believe her? He ruined shot after shot for the crew and was an obvious annoyance, yet he believed Rhonda was going to help him get on TV. Now *that*, people, is what we call Classic Narcissism! It also reminds us that most thugs, bullies and jerks — when left to their own devices — are *idiots*!

Here's something we've noticed over the years while training a lot of women. Many of us are so used to being good and honest with everyone, it would not even occur to us to *lie*, even to protect ourselves. Sure Rhonda lied to this young man... and he deserved it.

Ironically, in many cases lying may be the best strategy. It falls under the "Dissuasion" category of the 4D's. For example, if a sleazebag stops you in your neighborhood and asks "do you live around here?" it's absolutely OK to say "no, I'm on my way to visit my friend who's a cop."

So don't be fooled by a fool: listen for information, then stand up for yourself and set a boundary. What could it hurt? And who knows — you may just wind up with a better job for doing so, just like Rhonda... who was promoted to a paid position that very day.

R is for RELAXING

Relaxing might also seem like a strange topic for a personal safety book, but let us tell you why it makes sense. This concept is easy to understand when learning how to drive, or learning a new sports activity. Beginning drivers grip the steering wheel too hard, as if the strength of the grip will make them better drivers. A good driving instructor will tell them to relax their grip, as the tension doesn't translate into more control. The same is true of a sport. A tighter grip on a bat or golf club doesn't deliver the result you or your coach wants for the team.

Rhonda Responsible also remained relaxed and cool under pressure. She didn't explode at the guy, she didn't threaten him or even ask for a man to intervene; she just handled it herself, and we might add, quite effectively.

The same concept applies to learning self-defense. In general, it is easier to function when you are relaxed. If your body is tense and your muscles are tight, or you are moving around too much, you are not ready to respond as quickly to a threat as when you are relaxed. Human reaction time is about ¼ of a second. That means it takes your body about a ¼ of a second to respond to what your brain tells it to do. If you are relaxed, your response is quicker and smoother than if you are tense. In addition, if your muscles are tense your body has to first relax them before moving them, wasting precious time. All that can be avoided by staying as relaxed as you can in the moment.

In events involving people we don't know, which we call "stranger situations," the most common scenario is an assailant approaching his prospective victim and asking her a seemingly innocent question. We call this the "interview," and it's also part of the "Dissuasion" category of the 4D's we discussed previously. Because this is so important, we want to reiterate that this is your opportunity to *talk* your way out of the situation, your chance to show him you are not a good target. The more relaxed you are, the calmer you are. And the calmer you look, the more ominous you appear — making you an obviously bad choice for him.

In familiar situations, scenarios with people you know, staying relaxed keeps you calm and in control of the situation. When you are dealing with someone you know, you are more likely to be persuaded into an argument, but **the Safety Godmothers** know that arguing is no way to communicate. The way to have the advantage when dealing with everyday interpersonal communication is to remain calm, stick to the topic at hand and not get goaded into a fight. To do this effectively requires you to be relaxed. It's even the same for date-rape situations: remain relaxed and calm so you can think and stay in control, so you cannot be convinced to do something you are not comfortable doing.

You are now probably thinking "how am I supposed to stay relaxed when I'm afraid for my life or nervous about a confrontation?" **The Safety Godmothers** have some ideas about that. When you *know* you are capable of defending yourself, or of talking your way out of a situation, you are more able to remain relaxed in just about any circumstance. This is why we recommend — no, we *beg* — that you take some kind of self-defense course. We feel that any reputable empowerment-based class you take to feel more secure is important. However, all self-defense classes are not equal. We want you to read our criteria for selecting a self-defense class (it's at the end of the book) and encourage you to "shop" before you commit.

As you know by now, we also think it's important to practice verbal strategies as much as possible. If you cannot find a self-defense program in your area that trains for verbal inter-action, we recommend you get a group of friends and practice together. It may seem awkward or silly at first, but if you take it seriously, this can be very helpful.

Keep in mind that you have the advantage in most of these situations, because the coward who wants to accost you has the mistaken impression that you are weaker than he is and an easy target. He has likely attacked women before and is expecting a specific response. When you respond differently than he expects, you throw him off his script. The element of surprise is an important tool in your personal safety kit!

The Safety Godmothers know it is easier said than done, but with a little bit of practice you can learn to stay relaxed and in control in nearly any situation.

SUSAN STANDS HER GROUND

Susan was a nurse with lots of compassion for the sick and no patience for fools. She was tall, middle-aged, and not particularly athletic, although she was in pretty good shape. Her colleagues at the hospital in the high desert town of Palmdale, California, looked up to Susan — their friend and co-worker — because she was always in charge, in control, and walked tall with her head held high.

One dark, starlit evening on the overnight shift, Susan needed to walk outside from one building to the next. As she started to leave, one of the other nurses, in a noticeable state of fear and agitation, said, "Don't go outside… there are gang members sitting on the steps."

Susan said to her colleagues, "I will not be frightened by a group of thugs. And I don't have time to wait for the police to show up. I'm going out there." Little did the others know that Susan had taken a self-defense class the year before and was confident in both herself and her abilities.

As she approached the group sitting on the steps, she could smell the marijuana and the alcohol coming from their direction. As she approached, they looked at her with obvious disrespect and disdain. Susan realized that addressing the pot and booze issue might be pushing it, and decided to save it for the police. As she got closer, she made direct eye contact with them, and just as she got to the steps she pointed to each of them in turn and said, "You, you, you, and you, get off these steps and wait somewhere else... *now!*"

The tough looking gang-bangers took no time to decide; they all got up immediately and walked away without a comment or a second glance.

Susan kept an eye on them by watching their reflection in the window and then walked over to the hospital annex without looking back. The familiar smell of antiseptic stung her nose as she walked through the doors, and she took a deep sigh of relief.

HOW WE SEE IT

Susan was not intimidated. Fundamentally, Susan became the leader that most people thought she already was. We trust that, if Susan had felt the signs of *real* fear — like the hair on the back of her neck standing up or her stomach clenching — she would have not gone outside. As it was, she remembered what a lot of us have forgotten: elders and community members can wield authority, if they let themselves have it.

When we were growing up, there were neighbors who would not let us get away with bad behavior. We knew darn well our parents would find out if we were misbehaving. Susan brought a small town sensibility to a large city phenomenon, where teens frequently get away with bad and sometimes criminal behavior because they feel invisible. It's much easier to be anonymous in a big city. And sometimes, stepping in as Susan did makes an impact. These boys, gang affiliation or not, had respect for an older woman telling them what to do. This strategy fits into the "humanizing the potential perpetrator" category which we discussed in the 4D's.

We are by *no means* advocating going out and confronting gang members as a duty or obligation. That said, Susan set a boundary with these boys and pushed their "don't mess with grandma" buttons by telling them very directly what she wanted them to do.

Many women work in professions that involve one-on-one interaction with the so-called "public," which can potentially put them in harm's way. Some examples are real estate agents who drive strangers around or sit alone in open houses, flight attendants, mental health workers dealing with delirious patients who may be "off their meds," food service folks who work late hours, and cocktail servers and bartenders who serve people who drink.

We believe it should be mandatory that hospital employees and volunteers learn the basics of personal safety. Bacteria and viruses hurt people. People who are in pain themselves can also hurt people!

S is for SELF-DEFENSE

People often equate Karate, Jiu Jitsu, Tae Kwon Do or similar martial arts as self-defense, even though many others regard them as a sport. While these techniques *can* be used for self-defense, they are not what we do. We teach a system of self-defense that contains elements from many sources: street smarts, traditional martial arts, even time-tested techniques we've developed ourselves. But we don't expect people to understand the finer distinctions at first glance. That's why, after decades of experience, we are finally writing about our favorite topic. We're experts! We have taught thousands of people all over the US, and in other countries as well.

The most common view of self-defense is, not surprisingly, based on what people have seen in movies or on television. They think of it mostly as rooted in martial arts, or maybe they have a cartoonish memory of a 6th season "King of the Hill" episode where Bobby takes a class at the local YMCA, the one we mentioned in this book's Introduction.

Fundamentally, the people who take to self-defense like ducks to water are the people who have a strong sense of *self*. One needs a self to defend. For people who are used to being manipulated, coerced or cowed, self-defense is harder.

In the previous story, Susan had a super-strong experience of self and was able to not only defend herself but take action to make her surroundings safer; in this example, the hospital grounds.

We don't use "self-defense" in the name of our non-profit, IMPACT Personal Safety, although we definitely teach it. Personal safety is a larger field which encompasses self-defense because, while we do teach people how to physically fight back, we teach fighting *as a last resort* and emphasize setting verbal and physical boundaries BEFORE it actually goes to a fight. Many things other than fighting are involved with personal safety. WE TEACH YOU STUFF WE HOPE YOU NEVER HAVE TO USE!

Self-defense in its broadest sense is anything you do to keep yourself safe and away from harm; literally, the defense of one's self. In that context, you could say that applying liberal amounts of sunblock while at the beach is self-defense of one's skin. It's basic and simple, but it will protect you against skin cancer, which can be lethal.

One of our dreams is to have a physical self-defense component included in physical education classes as an "of course!" part of any curriculum. We see this as part of a bigger picture for people, which we call "physical literacy."

Physically literate people know basic rules about keeping themselves and their loved ones safe. We teach kids to look both ways when they cross the street. We teach them to know the meaning of traffic light colors. As passengers, there are personal safety rules that are often dictated by state laws: seat belts, child safety seats, etc. We all deal with personal safety rules on a daily basis. We learn food handling safety so we won't get sick or even die from improper food preparation. Physically literate people know to wash their hands before they cook for themselves and others.

When you learn how to drive, you learn how to do a potentially dangerous activity in the safest way possible. It's awkward at first, but by the time you've driven for a few months, it becomes part of you and feels natural. Soon, you'll never even think about it at all.

So far, physical or verbal self-defense is not considered as basic as traffic safety. We are out to change that. In Los Angeles and New York, we're proud to say that many private schools are seeing what an important piece self-defense is for their students. We have yet to make significant inroads into the more rigid, conservative — and severely cash-strapped — public school systems, but we are working on it.

We think that a lot of the resistance to learning self-defense skills lies with denial, and wishing the world would be different than it is. Some people feel they are succumbing to negativity by even *contemplating* taking a self-defense course, mistakenly thinking, "If I do this, I'll be no better than the low-life's I detest, and I'm better than that!" We, on the other hand, think that buying car insurance, learning to swim, washing your hands, and using a seat belt and understanding there are idiots on the road is *not* succumbing to negativity; instead, it is simply acknowledging there are risks to just being alive and going about day-to-day activities. It is taking responsibility for your life, at least as much as possible.

Similarly, while most people are not dangerous, there are people in the world who didn't get the "don't be violent" memo. The predators are there: they have always been there, and they will probably always be there. And they count on a big percentage of us being clueless about how to deal with them. We are committed to ending that, once and for all.

So we talk, we write books, we talk more (we talk a *lot*) and we enlist your help in getting the word out. You have a *right* to learn how to protect your own body from harm, and we have the document to prove it.

Article 3 of the abridged version of the United Nations Universal Declaration of Human Rights, adopted and proclaimed by the United Nations General Assembly in 1948 and reaffirmed by all of the governments of the world in 1993, states: "Every person has the right to life, liberty and *security of person.*"

We are the "liberty and security of person" people. As a matter of fact, the safety of people is pretty much all **the Safety Godmothers** ever think about.

We can't usher in the day when personal safety is thought of as a "normal" thing without your help. After reading this book, our sincerest wish is that you join us in making personal safety and self-defense as "normal" as learning to swim or taking driver's education. Look in the back of this book for ways you can help out, and make your voice heard.

TRACY TAKES HIM DOWN

Tracy had just finished her junior year of high school and was visiting her sister at an Ivy League University on the east coast. She had also just finished a self-defense class at her high school, and felt she could take care of herself in a dangerous situation. But she never imagined she would need to use her skills at a place like one of the "Big" schools.

One night Tracy went to a party with her sister. It was on campus at one of the fraternity houses. Tracy was walking from the back house across the lawn to the main house. As she did, she passed a drunk young man who leered at her while saying, "Hey there pretty girl, where you going so fast?"

The hair on the back of Tracy's neck stood on end, her heart started palpitating and she could feel the adrenaline surge — all the signs she'd been taught to recognize when danger was near. Tracy kept on walking. After a few yards, she was violently grabbed and shoved into the bushes by the same guy, who was now yelling "You can't just ignore me, bitch! Who do you think you are?"

Tracy was still on her feet, and could feel the branches tearing at her clothes and scratching her skin; she still could not believe it was happening. Her first thought was, "Oh great, I'm doing exactly what my teacher told us *not* to do: I'm at a frat party in a short skirt and high heels. I'm drinking and I'm separated from my friends…"

Then, as the guy started pulling up Tracy's skirt, she thought to herself, "This is *really happening…*" and that's when the training kicked in. In a flash, Tracy was back in class: she could hear her classmates yelling encouragement as they had done during her practice fights, and her instructor's voice coaching her. And then she wasn't thinking anymore — she had turned into a Punishment Machine. Tracy yelled "NO!" at the top of her lungs, then deftly delivered an eye strike followed by a well-placed knee to the groin, just like she had done to the padded assailants in class. Unfortunately for the attacker, he had no protective armor: he fell to the ground, immediately vomited, and Tracy ran into the frat house.

As soon as she got inside, Tracy found her sister and told her what happened. A call to campus security should have been the end of it, but what happened next defies even drunk logic. A few minutes later, the attempted rapist stumbled into the party, zeroed in on Tracy, threw his beer at her and called her a bitch. By this time *everyone* at the party had heard about what happened to Tracy but, if the perpetrator had not come back inside, Tracy would never have known who he was. Now that she could clearly identify him (along with everyone else), the police were called and the perpetrator was arrested.

HOW WE SEE IT

Wow! Wow! Wow! While we definitely wish that Tracy had been more cautious about drinking at a frat house, as you know, girls will be girls! Tracy did what she learned in her self-defense class, which a lot of untrained girls would be reluctant to do: *resist*, and resist *effectively*.

You'll notice that Tracy also drew upon self-talk that helped her get out of denial. Denial is present regardless of how much we *think* we won't deny what's happening to us. Denial is a mechanism that is useful for survival. After all, we can't walk around being terrified all the time, so we have to entertain a certain level of denial in order to function in the world.

That said, when the bushes and the scratching broke through Tracy's denial, her self-defense kicked in... literally and figuratively. She swiftly jabbed the assailant in the eyes, triggering the automatic flinch response that causes all humans to reflexively protect their eyes. Once the assailant naturally and immediately reacted to cover his face, it gave Tracy an opening to either do the next technique or get away — in this case, finishing him with a knee to the groin.

If the young man had not been so arrogant, he would have limped home with his bruised testicles and bruised ego, but NOOOOOOOO, he had to go into the party to "piss" on the woman who had hurt him. What an idiot! As you've no doubt already noticed in this collection of tales, ego is a large factor in male violence.

By the way, we are *not* saying that untrained girls can't or won't defend themselves; we just know that those who have practiced, like Tracy did, are more ready, willing and able to do so. Adrenaline-based training is a proven way to reduce injury and risk, so why not train people to prepare for possible human emergencies?

There is also a larger issue lurking in Tracy's story. If you are a college-bound person, you should know that the most common form of assault will be perpetrated by someone you are acquainted with. Tracy didn't know her assailant as she was simply visiting the campus, and was mentally prepared for a stranger encounter. However, we teach our students that the primary thing to mentally prepare for is to be willing to hurt the other person who is attempting to hurt them, whether a stranger *or* a familiar.

Please heed this important news story from freelance author Rod Bastenmehr for Alternet.com, which as of this writing was hot off the web.

"In January 2014, the White House released a report, authored by the Council on Women and Girls, called 'Rape and Sexual

Assault: A Renewed Call to Action.' The report says that 1 in 5 women have been sexually assaulted at their college or university, but that only a mere 12 percent of student victims report the assault. Further, while only 7 percent of college men *admit* they have attempted rape, 63 percent of those men have been involved in multiple assaults, averaging 6 each." Bastenmehr adds, "And those are just the ones that admit it." You can download the full PDF of the White House report at tinyurl.com/m6t3spr and also access a variety of resources. (For more info, see the References pages in the Appendix at the back of this book.)

President Obama declared it is a White House priority to impact pervasive sexual assaults, as seen in this speech from January 2014: tinyurl.com/WH-Priority. The president especially calls upon men to step up and be proactive with other men in stopping violence against women.

Once you are at college, there are actions you can take to help shift the rape culture. Encourage friends to take a self-defense class, encourage everyone to report assaults, and engage the men and boys on campus to be a part of the solution rather than part of the problem.

An outstanding action to take is to book either a speaker or a full-blown seminar by *Girls Fight Back*; go to www. girlsfightback.com and click on the SEMINARS tab.

There are even actions you can take if you're still in grade school or middle school. For example, if you're active in Girl Scouts, encourage your troop to take on self-defense as a Badge activity, or find out if one of Anea Bogue's *REALgirls* seminars is available in your area by visiting her site at www. aneabogue.com/realgirl/ and calling the contact number listed there.

Sexual assault is not a women's issue; it is a *human* issue that affects everyone. Tracy was truly victorious for herself and others. We're pretty confident that Mr. Bruised Man On Campus had his rape career severely nipped in the bud that night. We'd like to nip his bud in other ways, but that's a whole other commentary.

T is for TACHYPSYCHIA

"Tachypsychia" — as defined on the Wikipedia, and pronounced tak-ee-sike-ee-uh — is a neurological condition that alters the perception of time, usually induced by physical exertion, drug use, or a traumatic event.

In *Tracy Takes Him Down* we observe that Tracy had a moment when everything appeared to slow down, allowing her to have a conversation with herself: "Oh great, I'm doing exactly what my teacher told us *not* to do: I'm at a frat party in a short skirt and high heels. I'm drinking and I'm separated from my friends…" And then, "this is *really happening*…" It seemed like a long time for her, but in reality, it was only seconds. Once her denial switched off and her survival instinct kicked in — she even heard her classmates cheering for her — she fought for her life and won!

A non-danger example of tachypsychia would be at the ice rink. It's not uncommon to hear ice skaters, who are competing for the first time in the Olympics, say about their 4 ½ minute routine, "it all went by in a flash!" if they aced it. Conversely, if they made terrible and costly mistakes, they'll often say "my routine seemed to go on forever. I couldn't wait for it to be over."

We experience tachypsychia whenever we are adrenalized. Some people refer to this experience as the fight-or-flight response; it is the body getting ready to defend itself against, or flee from, the danger. The adrenal medulla produces the hormone epinephrine (a.k.a. adrenaline) and releases it into the bloodstream along with dopamine and norepinephrine, resulting in several physiological responses.

People usually refer to increased strength and a higher tolerance for pain when talking about adrenaline, but there is so much more that occurs. Your perception of time changes: it either lengthens, making events appear to slow down, or contracts, making events appear to be moving very quickly. Your heart beats faster and your blood pressure rises, as blood flows away from your extremities and in toward your center mass, giving your vital organs extra oxygen for increased performance. Your bronchial passages dilate allowing your body to absorb more of much-needed oxygen. Your pupils dilate, allowing more light to enter, and visual exclusion occurs allowing greater focus.

The downside of that focus is the loss of peripheral vision, or what is often called "tunnel" vision. When you experience tunnel vision, all you can really see is what is directly in front of you, and you tend to lock your focus on that one thing.

And the hits just keep on comin': along with the visual effect, auditory exclusion also occurs, muffling some sounds and amplifying others. Your body even produces and releases extra glucose, giving you an energy boost.

It is because of tachypsychia that we have our students step back after the fight, and shake off the tunnel vision by looking around to see if there is someone who can help them, to see if safety is close by, to see if the assailant has someone with him, and to make sure they aren't in the middle of the street about to get hit by a bus. At this point, if you are in a populated area, you would just run for safety. If you are out hiking or in some other secluded location, you have to make sure he doesn't get up and come after you, so you move toward the top of the assailant's head — but further than 2 arm's lengths away — and check to make sure he's not getting up soon. Then you run for help — for *yourself*, not for him!

That all sounds great, but — on the other side of an adren-aline surge — people have also reported that when they were attacked, they couldn't move, couldn't think, couldn't even *breathe*; this is the freeze response. In our classes, it is our goal to reduce the length of the freeze response so we experience only a short "assessment period" rather than a longer freeze. As it relates to personal safety, reason, logic and fine-motor movements are not available when you are highly adrenalized — *unless* you have been trained using scenario-based, adrenal response training. It's the same reason that "first-responders" (fire and police personnel, EMTs, etc.) drill *constantly*, reproducing as closely as possible the scenarios they are likely to face. The more they drill, the less likely they are to freeze when the real thing happens.

Early on in class, our students often don't remember what they did in their fights: they can't recall the fight itself or what the mugger said to them. We'll see them watching a tape of their fight almost slack-jawed, with a look of "did I really *do* that?" on their faces. Other students may feel like they were uncoordinated in their fight. But as we progress in the class, they get better at fighting and they start remembering their fights. They are even able to hold a conversation under high adrenal stress, a very special skill to have.

This is completely relatable to your everyday life. For example: remember when you had a disagreement with someone? After the disagreement, how many times have you thought "I'm such a dope! I should have said…" or "next time, I'm going to say…" Don't beat yourself up; it happens *so* often. There's nothing wrong with you, and it's understandable that you weren't able to say something pithy in the moment, or fire off the perfect come-back zinger. What happened is this: you experienced a low level of adrenaline that skewed your responses. It's the same when you are nervous about speaking up in class or giving a report; even low levels of adrenaline can slow down your perspective or response time. That's why it's important to practice things that make you nervous. Through practice, you get used to what you are doing, and you learn to manage the adrenaline while under stress.

Tachypsychia is a result of an adrenaline dump into your system. If you learn to manage your adrenaline, it will become an ally and an advantage, rather than a detriment and a disadvantage to you in both dangerous *and* safe situations.

USHER, OH NO U WON'T!

Usher is a very handsome young gay man living in West Hollywood, a known enclave for the LGBT community in Southern California. At only 18, he had already become somewhat jaded about attracting unwanted attention as he walked down the street. This day was really no different, except he was not in the mood to deal with anything or anyone. There had been a recent attack on a gay man in the neighborhood, so everyone was on edge about strange cars with men cruising around looking to cause trouble.

It was a beautiful spring day. As Usher walked home from the gym, he noticed a blue Camaro pacing him. He tried pretending to not notice the car, but became more annoyed as he got closer to home. Finally, he'd had enough. Having taken our Men's

Basics class, he knew it was better to face a possible problem than ignore it. Usher stopped and turned to look at the guy driving the car, extended his hands in frustration, shrugged and said "What?!" with as much attitude as he could muster.

The driver of the car started yelling and cursing at Usher, using all forms of hateful terms.

"Oh great," Usher thought, "Now what have I done?" He got into ready stance and began to de-escalate the situation as he'd learned and practiced in class.

"Look, I don't want any trouble. I'm just trying to walk home." The driver responded with "Well, you've *got* trouble now, faggot!"

At this point Usher just wanted to run home to his roommates, slam the door and set the alarm, but he knew that was a bad idea. He didn't want the potential basher to know where he lived, so he started walking again, this time toward the busier section of his neighborhood where he knew others would be around.

All the while the man followed him, screaming at him from the driver's seat. Soon, a neighbor saw what was happening and asked if Usher needed help. "Yes, please call 911," Usher responded. He continued down the street as the neighbor went in to make the call. Later, Usher would say he didn't feel a real threat until the guy actually pulled over and got out of his car.

The potential gay basher was now standing right in front of Usher, and said, "I'm gonna kill you, queer."

Usher, in ready stance and calmer than he'd ever thought possible, said in a quiet voice, "Oh, no... you won't."

Then, as if on cue, a black and white West Hollywood police car turned the corner.

Usher smiled to himself and laughed at the irony of being so happy to see the police arrive, when so often he'd feared them for being homophobic, a stereotype in law enforcement.

The assailant turned quickly and got back into his car, then sped off with the police in hot pursuit.

HOW WE SEE IT

Our dream is to see self-defense classes in every LGBT community everywhere, because hate crimes against non-hetero people continue to occur with tragic frequency. Under-reported, the FBI states that in 2008, out of more than 1600 homosexual hate crimes 58% were of an anti-male homosexual bias and 12% of an anti-female homosexual bias, with fewer non-specified for bi-sexual, transgendered, etc. It's no doubt gotten worse since then.

Our culture does not help, because it's still OK to bandy about "queer" insults meant to hurt. Sadly, epithets related to sexual identity are very common, starting in grade school where bullies get their bully careers started. Frequently, young bullies — both boys and girls — hurl painful terms like "queer," "faggot," "lesbo" and "dyke" toward the kids they victimize. Ideally our classes would be available not only to LGBT groups, but to kids who need to learn how to stop bullies on the playground and in school hallways. And we firmly believe that if bullies get stopped early on, they won't be cruising communities like West Hollywood when they are older.

Usher was very brave to face his pursuer, especially since he was aware of the news about the gay bashers who were still at large. Frankly, we think the term "bashing" softens and minimizes the true nature of these hate crimes. Bashing-Schmashing! There is no question about it: these are *attacks* and *assaults*.

We're not sure if the police ever caught the driver who harassed Usher. Since Usher didn't personally make the phone call to 911, there was no way for him to follow up with the dispatcher. If the cops did find and stop the driver, who knows how many assaults and batteries Usher prevented by simply asking his neighbor to call 911? We'll never know.

What we *do* know, however, is that Usher turned a very scary situation into something he was able to handle calmly… and with style, too.

U is for UNLADYLIKE

Chris Rock, the comedian, has a bit in one of his stand-up acts, the gist of which is: "I like going to strip clubs, but I don't want my daughter to work in one!" But c'mon, we're all *someone's* daughter. Men and boys want women and girls to be sexy and to take their clothes off or dress provocatively, but they devalue the women who do. We are caught between a (Chris) rock and a hard place with this concept, sometimes referred to as the "Madonna / Whore" complex. Many young girls also get caught in this trap, which can take many forms. It is commonly called the double standard and it's alive and well. Watch for it.

In order to be popular, we do things that get us labeled a "bad girl," but once the boys are ready to move on and get married, they are not looking at the "bad girls" anymore; they look for "ladies." Now, we are not saying you should act a certain way so you can get married... we *are* saying that, as women and girls, we should be held to the same standards as men and boys: no more, no less.

Who decided what was "ladylike" anyway? And when did they decide it, and why is it important that we act that way? These are good questions to think about. As women, we have gone through some serious social evolution over time. At the dawn of humanity, women joined men in hunting and gathering. And while the male of the species may be physically stronger than the female, that did not exclude the females from this vital part of early life. Imagine a cave woman not able to defend herself... unlikely. For those women that stayed in the village, part of their job was keeping it safe while the others hunted. Then, at some point, we became "civilized" and women were no longer part of the hunting and gathering process. We became chattel to be owned, fought over, and protected. This is where we lost our fighting spirit.

Some historians surmise this is also where the insanity of gender inequality began. Over the last 25 years that we have been doing this work, we are happy to say things are starting to swing back to some semblance of sanity. As women in developed countries, we are not "owned" anymore and we are free to make our own life choices. We can decide what is "ladylike" for us as individuals.

Let's change the meaning of "ladylike" to include a girl or woman who knows how to take care of herself!

"No matter what the fight, don't be ladylike! God almighty made women and the Rockefeller gang of thieves made the ladies." — Mother Jones, Labor Organizer 1837-1930

VENICE VANQUISHERS

Three girls were walking along the boardwalk at Venice Beach, California, on a magnificent summer day. They knew each other very well and were having a great time simply being young. The ocean breeze tugged at their long blonde tresses, as the sounds and smells of the Hare Krishna's, street performers and incense hawkers followed them down the boardwalk. The sea birds wheeled overhead and competed with the hunks working out at Muscle Beach; you know… just a normal day in L.A.

The girls were distracted by all of it: the sounds and smells, the people, the stores. They had just gotten henna tattoos on their hips and were continuing down the boardwalk with their t-shirts rolled up to let the tattoos dry. They had been talking to people all day: vendors, locals, tourists, all pleasant exchanges. So they were caught off-guard when they were approached by a big, sloppy drunk man in his 40s sorely in need of some manners.

"Woo-hoo!" he screamed at one of the girls. "You are *hot*, baby!"

The girls continued to walk while keeping an eye on the louse, but not stopping.

"Ahh, c'mon, just talk to me. Me and my boys were wondering what kinda jeans those are…"

Sloppy Drunk Guy kept at it, and the girls felt like they were being sniffed by a dog. Finally, he got too close to one of the girls. She whirled on him — hands up in ready stance and game face on — and said in a very direct tone, "You need to leave *now!*"

Sloppy Drunk Guy let out a little yelp and ran away. The girls did not see him or his supposed friends again.

HOW WE SEE IT

First of all, do guys really think "Woo-hoo, you are *hot*, baby!" is a good pick-up line? Really? If that actually has worked, we'd love to hear about it.

If you think about it, young women are in almost as much of a bind — fashionably speaking — as their sisters from the past who had to wear corsets. OK, maybe not. Some of the young women who were forced to wear corsets actually had ribs surgically removed so they could have smaller, wispier waists. They endured those broken ribs, as mothers and sisters pulled the corset strings too tight, too fast. Their peers and parents would constantly warn, "No one wants to marry a fat woman!" Oh wait, we *do* have a lot of things in common with the past! But we digress.

The point is this: through the ages, young women are especially damned if they do and damned if they don't wear trendy fashions. They are teased if they aren't fashionable, yet are often blamed for being too suggestive in their clothing choices.

The three girls were dressed as teen girls dress; even though their rolled up t-shirts were modest compared to the ultra-skimpy bikinis and bathing suits that are in ample supply at Venice Beach, where the men also strut their... stuff. The girls' choice to roll up their t-shirts so the henna wouldn't stain their shirts was completely appropriate within the context of the time and place.

The inappropriate player in this little beach "drama" was Sloppy Drunk Guy. He had a scenario in mind that did not include them setting a boundary or standing up to him. He was dishing it out, and he sorely needed something to stop him. Our hero stopped his creepy behavior in a way that most teen girls would be too embarrassed or reluctant to try, even if they wanted to. But we know that if a woman puts up any kind of effective defense, the assailant will usually flee. That includes yelling — very loudly — "I don't know this man, I need help!" or simply standing up to him and setting a boundary as one of our three girls did. We drill verbal skills in our IMPACT classes in high schools because, when people feel uncertain or possibly threatened, it's hard to think of what to say.

We know it's vital to practice saying what you want, whether it's in a stressful situation like a job interview, or a recreational situation with drunken creeps. Hey, we prepare for ocean landings on flights from New York to Los Angeles where there's no water in between; why not prepare for handling a cretinous beach bum?

On a final note, if "Woo-hoo, you are *hot*, baby!" is the best opening line he can come up with, be grateful he let you know from the beginning that he's an idiot and not worth your time!

V is for VERBAL STRATEGIES

We Safety Godmothers are practical people; we want to get out of, or end, a dangerous situation without breaking a sweat…or a fingernail! Our philosophy is: once you know that you can defend yourself, you will be better able to talk your way out of a situation. We know people are more willing to act in their own defense if they believe they have a chance. Since most girls and women have been raised to think we couldn't possibly defend ourselves against a man, we just freeze because of a mistaken belief there is nothing we can do. Poppycock!

Even if you have not had the chance to take a full force, adrenaline based self-defense class, if you have just a little bit of faith in yourself — just a tiny bit of confidence, just a smidge of fighting spirit — you *can* defend yourself… AND you can talk your way out of most situations that are foreign to you with just a few tools. We recommend you practice those tools *before* you're in a circumstance where you need them.

To begin with — if you remember our section on the 4D's — the first thing you do in an uncertain situation is figure out the dynamics. To determine the dynamics, you have to observe his behavior, listen to what he's saying, figure out what he wants; then you can decide on a strategy.

So ask yourself these questions:

- "What is going on with him? (Is he angry, crazy, creepy, drunk or on drugs, nervous, suave?)
- "What is going on around me?"
- "Can someone help me; can I get to safety?"
- "What is he saying? And how shall I respond?"

In other words, what can you *say* that will make a difference? Turn his approach into a dialogue when he engages you.

To reiterate what we've said previously, we call this phase of a potential attack "The Interview." The potential assailant / interviewer talks to you to determine if you are a good choice for an assault or robbery, or whatever he has in mind. Your job is to look, and sound, like a bad choice for him to attack. If he is angry or crazy, you want to calm him down and convince him to let you leave. If he is creepy, drunk or nervous, you will most likely set a boundary that gets him to leave.

Enough generalizing... let's get specific! Here are some things you can do to talk your way out of just about any unnerving situation before it spirals out of control.

VERBAL STRATEGIES used by YOU, the DEFENDER

Tell a Lie

Never give vital information about yourself to someone you don't know or trust. Realize that you do not have to tell the truth to a stranger.

Creep: "Are you alone? Can I buy you a drink?"

You: "No, I'm meeting my friends here. They'll be along any minute." (Lie.)

Creep: "I'm lost. Can you help me?"

You: "I don't know the place you are looking for. Ask the officer around the corner." (Lie.)

Give specific directions (set a boundary)

This is the strategy used by the *Venice Vanquishers*. It is simple, direct and to the point: "Finally, he got too close to one of the girls. She whirled on him — hands up in ready stance and game face on — and said in a very direct tone 'You need to leave *now!*'"

Use directive-based, authoritative tones and stance:

- "Stop right there. Don't come any closer."
- "Back off. Turn around and walk away."
- "I want you to go away *now.*"
- "No, I am *not* coming with you."

De-escalate

Use calming, non-threatening tones and stance:

- "Look, I don't want any trouble."
- "We don't have to get into this."
- "Let's talk about it. We don't need to fight."
- "Stop yelling so we can discuss this."

It's effective to move back and forth between de-escalatory language and clear directive language to steer a situation away from a flashpoint, like this:

- "I need you to calm down. We can fix this if you stop yelling."
- "Take a step back and let's sit down."
- "I want to help. I don't want any trouble."
- "Back up and stop yelling so we can talk about this."

Deflect

- "I can't help you, but the security guard is right around the corner… SECURITY!!"
- "I can't help you, but I can call 911 for you…"

Cause a scene and attract the attention and help of others

Call out loudly and clearly, "I need help. I don't know this man. He's wearing..." and begin describing his attire.

Humanize

- "Hey, haven't I seen you before? Don't I know you?" or "I think I know your sister..."
- "Look, I don't even know you, I've never harmed you. Please just let me walk away."
- "What if this were happening to your sister..."

Empathize

- "You look scared. Are you nervous? You know, we don't have to do this."
- "Are you hungry (cold, tired)? You know, there is a shelter and soup kitchen right down the street..."
- "You seem angry, and I can understand why. You don't have to take it out on me. There are other ways..."

Verbal strategies will stay with you much better, longer and get stronger if you practice them, even in a mirror. A lot of women and girls are socialized to be uncomfortable with making unambiguous requests, so don't feel funny if practicing feels funny. That's why you practice *anything*. Once you've mastered these techniques, you can talk your way into safety whenever possible without breaking a sweat... or a nail.

WENDY WINDOW WINGER

Wendy drove home from work as she did every evening at 5:00 pm. She pulled up to the security gate where she had to use her keycard to gain entrance to the underground parking area at her apartment complex in West Hollywood, California.

As she rolled down her window, she caught a whiff of strong body odor, and then a man's arm reached in and tried to grab her around the throat. Wendy pushed the button to roll up her electric window, tightly trapping the erstwhile strangler's arm. She then threw the car into reverse, backed out of the driveway, and proceeded to drive down the street with her assailant's arm still stuck in the window. He, of course, was running beside the car while yelling, "Please lady, let me go!"

Wendy finally rolled down the window and the

assailant fell to the ground, "winged" as it were. Just imagine how much it must have hurt to have your arm rolled up in an electric car window! She drove immediately to the police station and made a report.

The police came to Wendy's apartment building to check things out. As they were canvassing the building, they heard a woman screaming. When they went to investigate, they found the same man had broken into another woman's apartment and was attempting to assault *her*. We wonder if he tried to get in through a window.

Once he was arrested and booked, it turned out he was wanted for multiple rapes in the area.

HOW WE SEE IT

Well done, Wendy! As proven here, it is of critical importance to be *super* aware whenever you pull up to an entrance that requires a code or card access. Perpetrators have figured out that you are vulnerable. This concept was vividly proven here, as the Ass-ailant — another fellow worthy of removal from the gene pool — was "lying in wait." That said, Wendy did not hesitate one second to use her window as a Weapon of Ass Destruction!

Note: when you are driving a rental car, make sure you acquaint yourself with all of the controls and where they are in case you need to use them quickly. When you are in your own car, you have naturally developed a muscle memory and don't have to think about where the locks, window controls or light switches are. Wendy was able to hit the window control quickly because her body already knew where it was.

Also, Good Thinking Points are awarded for giving the guy the "run around." Of course, we would have loved it if she'd just gone right to the police station, with him still running alongside her car. That is *really* the stuff dreams are made of — at least, ours! As we have already duly noted, this story underscores that criminals are often one spark plug short of a well running car.

And then to top if off, this guy's arm must have hurt like the dickens, but he thinks, "What the hell? As long as I'm out, I might as well try one more assault today!" Figuring out the machinations of the Criminal Mind is always perplexing, yet in its own way weirdly entertaining.

Typically, rapists are often multi-offenders, and while current statistics are hard to come by, an early 90's report says that 67% of convicted rapists are repeat offenders. Sadly, there is no reason to believe that number has gone done in the last 20 years.

Wendy's resistance saved at least one other woman in her apartment from rape, and undoubtedly many others. Thank goodness Wendy had her wits about her the whole time. Thanks to her, the only window the assailant will be sticking his arm through will have bars on it.

W is for WEAPONS

People always ask us "What if he has a weapon?" **The Safety Godmothers** have many thoughts about this hot-button topic. Most people ask this question because they have the erroneous notion that an assault will most likely involve a weapon... however, it turns out the opposite is true! According to Susan Wilde's *Worth Defending* website (tinyurl.com/Wilde-Worth), and based on mid-90s FBI statistics:

"In rapes / attempted rapes / sexual assaults: 84% were unarmed, 6% used a firearm, and 10% used an edged or blunt weapon. There's a very good chance that if you're assaulted, you won't have to contend with a weapon. Next, if someone walks up to you with a weapon and does not use it on you, you have the chance to talk your way out of the situation. The assailant usually prefers to use the weapon as a tool of threat and intimidation. That being said, an armed assailant is dangerous and you must tread carefully."

By the way, a more recent National Crime Victimization Study in 2010 (tinyurl.com/NCVS-2010) now puts the percentage of rapists using *any* kind of weapon at 11%. This means the odds of dealing with a weapon are going *down*. And yet, rapes depicted in movies and on TV typically involve a weapon, leading women to think this is the norm. Not so!

Even though the probability of encountering a weapon during an assault is relatively low, that doesn't mean it can't happen. We all know it can. This is why IMPACT Personal Safety offers a more advanced Weapons Class, which you can take after completing the 20 Hour Women's

Basics course. In this class, students learn how to disarm knife, club or gun-wielding assailants, and the best ways to protect themselves.

Also covered are weapons *you* can use, ones that are all around us. We suggest you look around and see what in your environment could be used as a weapon. We teach you in our classes to use your body as a weapon, but also... hey, look at that lamp — it's not just for illumination anymore! Used to bonk someone on the head if you get the chance, it becomes a head-bonker. The iron that *Julie Justice* had thrown at her by her former boyfriend? Weapon. *Wendy Window Winger* used her car window as a weapon to entrap and lead her erstwhile assailant away and down the street.

On the other side of the coin, if someone comes up to you with a weapon, it's important to first determine his motivation: what does he want? If he wants your stuff, he can have it. You can get more things or more money; there's no need to get hurt over something you can replace. In most cases, the robber will take whatever he's asked for and be on his way.

If he wants you to come along with him, that is a different story altogether. Most of the time, assailants are armed because they are afraid you won't cooperate if they *don't* have a weapon. Your best tool here is negotiation.

Keep in mind that the assailant is choosing you in the first place because, for some reason, you look like a good target to him — someone who will not fight back. He is choosing someone he perceives as weaker than he is. Then he adds a weapon because he does not feel confident enough to handle the situation alone, and the weapon he chooses is the one he feels is most intimidating. Basically that means he himself is afraid of that weapon. This is important information; it might give you the psychological upper-hand.

We *strongly* discourage going with someone in their car, even if he is armed. We cannot express this fervently enough: **it's not going to get better if you go with him.**

People often think, "If I just do what the assailant is telling me to do, it will be fine." But it is almost *never* fine. Do you really expect the man who is holding a weapon on you to be honest with you when he says, "If you just do what I say, you'll be fine. I won't hurt you." I mean, c'mon, the man means you nothing but harm and you think he's going to suddenly become a stand-up guy? No way.

Repeat after us: **DO NOT GET INTO THE CAR**. You have a greater chance of survival if you refuse to get into the car. Instead, cause a scene — what assailant wants everyone in the area looking at him? — or run away. *Just don't get into the car even if it's your own car.*

Now you may ask, "what if things get out of control, and he shoots me?" While not pleasant, the answer is simple: if he shoots you in the grocery store parking lot, you have a better chance of survival than if he takes you out to the middle of nowhere. If you get shot or stabbed in the parking lot, someone will be able to help you, but if it happens out in the middle of the desert, there will be *no one* there to help you.

While we're on this topic, here's a repulsive but fascinating statistic most people don't know: according to a 2006 *New York Times* article, if a gunshot victim's heart is still beating by the time they arrive at the hospital, they have a 95% chance of survival!

This may seem like a weird thing to be happy about, but think about it. Most people think that if they get shot, they will die, so they comply with someone whose intention is clearly malevolent because they think their odds will improve. But the truth is you are more likely to survive getting shot in a public area than if you go somewhere with a stranger. *Period.* (For proof, see the "Surviving Gunshot Wounds" entry in the *References* section at the end of the book.)

In a rape scenario, it could go a couple of ways. You might be able to talk him into putting the weapon away, then fight like normal. Or if he puts the weapon down, you might pick it up, fling it away and *then* fight. But it is unlikely that he can hold the weapon on you while undressing himself and possibly you while maneuvering around the situation — and let's not forget, he will be handling his most prized possession at the same time! It's unlikely that he would use a knife or gun so close to his family jewels, if you know what we mean... so he will have to put the weapon down at some point, giving you an opening.

And yes, we know there are exceptions. There are always exceptions to *everything.*

Caveat: The use of guns and other weapons is beyond the scope of this book. However, should your family choose to have a weapon at home, please know and tell your parents that handling and firing a gun of any kind requires regular and continual practice and training. When you are dealing with any kind of lethal weapon, the user must be prepared to keep their skills sharp.

The main thing here is that when a weapon is introduced, the stakes go up. That's true whether you are at the receiving or delivering end of that weapon. However, when you are facing someone with a weapon, that doesn't automatically mean you can't have the advantage or save your life.

XAVIER, SELF-SAVIOR

Xavier was a husband, father and grandfather in his early 80s. He had a Bucket List of things he wanted to do before he "kicked the bucket." He always dreamed of going through the Panama Canal, of hearing the New York Philharmonic, of visiting Istanbul. His wife did not like travel, so Xavier decided he would travel on his own.

He disembarked from his luxury cruise ship when it arrived at Istanbul. He had not bonded with any of the other passengers, so despite admonitions to stay in groups, Xavier struck out on his own. He couldn't wait to drink in the sights and sounds of one of the most famous cities in the world. He longed to smell the grilling meats and spices in the market places and to see the famous Byzantine mosaics.

Just as Xavier left the ship, a Turkish man approached

him, cigarette burning closely to his fingers. He asked Xavier if he would like to see some fine "cheap" souvenirs. Xavier did not want to hurt the man's feelings, or to seem like he was prejudiced against swarthy-looking Turkish men. Xavier wanted to fight his own bias against the stereotype of scary foreigners, so he dutifully followed the man.

In a few moments they were winding their way down narrow streets and alleyways, getting farther away from the ship and safety. Xavier realized what was happening and said to himself, "I'm an idiot," recognizing that he had become a classic "mark"; Xavier also realized how vulnerable he now was. He had never encountered a potentially violent situation in his home state of Iowa, but he'd seen plenty of movies over the years. He searched his mental "data bank" and decided he needed to give his ersatz tourist guide the slip.

Just as in the movies, Xavier looked for a darkened doorway. As soon as he found one, and could see that the man was not looking, he stepped over the threshold and hid behind some curtains. He waited there until he felt he was safe, then very carefully looked both ways as he stepped out onto the street. He made it back to the ship in plenty of time to sign up for a tour with other people.

HOW WE SEE IT

We don't know about you, but this story made us nervous. We found ourselves saying out loud, "No, don't follow him!" But we are so happy that Xavier's intuition kicked in and he followed it… whew!

Cruises are common vacations for the elderly because they feel safer on a ship, with most of their activities located onboard and in groups. We think it's a bad idea for *anyone* — young or old — to get off a ship and visit a foreign city on their own, but traveling in groups makes sense to us.

In this story, Xavier did what we are so used to women and girls doing: putting himself in danger so as not to hurt the other person's feelings. But he quickly realized his mistake and took action.

Finally, we often complain about the misinformation about violence that we get from movies and TV, and while we don't advocate hiding as a primary self-defense strategy, there are times in which hiding may make sense, as it did for Xavier in this story. He imitated a smart evasion move that he had seen in films and was able to get away to safety.

But not all examples of hiding in movies are a good idea, For example, in most slasher movies, when the crazy machete-wielding, back-from-the-dead, woman-killer comes after the baby-sitter, you know darn well that she should not hide up in the attic or down to the basement! But of course she does. (Doesn't she ever *watch* slasher movies?) The reasons we think hiding from danger, especially in your home, is a bad idea are two-fold:

1. Unless you have a hidden door leading to a secret tunnel or a panic room that is impervious to break-ins, there

probably isn't one place to hide in your house that someone else wouldn't think about or stumble upon.

2. Hiding puts the other person in control. By hiding, by being passive, you are waiting for them to find you, and whatever happens will happen on their terms. We recommend leaving your house by a back door or window and getting help from a neighbor.

For those who can't take a self-defense class for health or other reasons, movies and TV are usually all they've got. Thankfully, Xavier had remembered a move based in reality, not fantasy.

X is for the X FACTOR

A major frustration for **the Safety Godmothers** are the frequent requests we get from the media for superficial tips or rules concerning self-defense. Broadcast media people *really* like lists of short, catchy "how-to's" or "If (fill in the blank) happens, what should our viewers or listeners do? Give us a list of TIPS!"

The major tip *we've* got? Turn off the often misleading and fear-inducing news programs and enroll in a self-defense class!

Seriously though, a request for tips implies a rigidity that can be deceptive when confronted with danger or potentially dangerous circumstances. This is also known as the "X Factor" or more commonly, the unknown. There are very few "snappy pointers" that will work *every time* under all circumstances, and having handy-dandy simplistic rules and platitudes can actually hurt people more than help them.

In the story of "Xavier, Self-Savior" we see that at least one common sense tip we all know — don't go anywhere with a stranger in a foreign country — went right out the window when Xavier was actually in the moment.

We especially hate, hate, *hate* the almost semi-annual barrage of email collections of "Personal Safety Tips" that get sent around by well-meaning but clueless people. By the time most folks get done reading the so-called rules, they are generally more scared than before they started reading them. The tips are usually based on things *not* to do instead of positive actions to take. So here's another major tip: don't read those email tips and for goodness' sakes, don't share them!

While learning anything, whether it's gymnastics, piano, or

even self-defense, there actually *are* simple rules or tips at play, but many are unspoken: pay attention, listen to your gut, watch people who are better than you are. However, the true sign of mastery is the ability to improvise in the moment with the basic tools and rules we teach and practice, because life is messy and rarely follows a formula. What we aspire to do is train you to deal with X, the factor that is unknown.

Let's be clear: we're not actually against tips and rules … just *stupid* tips and rules, or tips and rules that are used by others — such as the media — as shortcuts to circumvent actual training. We often use the swimming analogy for the larger topic of self-defense. As we've noted before, swimming is a form of self-defense, but with water instead of unruly people. With swimming, there are definitely some rules and tips: holding your breath while underwater is a good one. Don't pretend to be drowning as a ruse to get the lifeguard to notice you. Don't use a butterfly stroke in a crowded pool, etc.

Similarly, with self-defense, here's our best and possibly most paradoxical tip, which the media studiously avoids: "the best fight is none at all." Also stated as "the best way to win a fight is to not be in one." Don't fight unless absolutely necessary. Second tip: "if you choose to fight, give it everything you've got!"

Here are a few more reliable tips that we've covered so far, so we can get back to our discussion of "X," the unknown:

- Be aware of your surroundings.
- Believe your intuition; if someone or something gives you the creeps, don't talk yourself out of it.
- Don't let anyone else bamboozle you into ignoring your own gut, whether it's a dare or someone making fun of you.

Now to the X Factor, and back to the swimming analogy. If you are a strong swimmer, you know the rules and you know yourself, your body, and your confidence level. You can look at a body of water and decide, "That is too rough for my current skills." You bring an informed and trained eye to the circumstances. You can see that you and the rough water — the X in the swimmer scenario — are not a good match.

Learning self-defense is similar. Once you understand that predators are flesh and blood just like you, and that a hulking man's eyeballs are the same as yours and just as vulnerable, you begin to forget the "bad tips" we've been raised with and factor in your own strengths, experience and courage.

Many of us have been raised to be afraid of any and all men as a way to stay safe. That's as misinformed as someone being afraid of any and all water. If you don't know how to swim and are afraid of water, even the smallest, safest-looking wading pool looks scary and possibly deadly. What the non-swimmer — and by extension, the "defenseless" person — has not been trained to address is the X Factor: the unknown.

That's where we come in. We level the playing field by training our students to find and act on X Factors. We train people to see predators as human beings who make mistakes, who have weaknesses, and who can be defended against.

The real X factor then becomes *you*, the wild card a predator didn't factor in at all. Pretty cool!

YOLANDA, YOU'RE NOT DRIVING!

West Hollywood is a friendly, upscale community with neighbors who like to get involved; the crime rate is low because people are vigilant and, well… a bit intrusive. Yolanda, still in high school and a proud self-defense class graduate, loved being a part of the community. One late summer afternoon she heard a commotion outside her workplace. As she looked outside the door to see what was going on, a couple of people shouted for her to come out and help. Being a "Good Samaritan" type, she decided to join the group to see what she could do.

There were three young women and one young man who were embroiled in a noisy confrontation. Bystanders in West Hollywood usually do more than just gawk, and that was the case here. They had already called the police; when one of the girls ran off crying, a neighbor went after her to make sure she would not run into traffic.

As it turns out, the quartet was visiting from Eagle Rock, a distant suburb about 20 miles from West Hollywood, and it was time to drive home. The problem was the driver and car owner — the only male in the group — was both drunk *and* high. Even though Yolanda was yards away she could still smell the alcohol. The girls were pleading with him to give them the keys, so one of them could drive. Of course he was resisting.

As Yolanda stood back to assess the situation, two of the young women got into the car to wait for the girl who had run away to return. Suddenly, and with surprising speed, Zonked Guy got into the driver's seat and started the car. Without missing a beat, Yolanda walked up to the driver's side, opened the door, and said, "Turn off the car, get out and give me the keys... *now!*" He complied immediately with no hesitation whatsoever.

Yolanda said to the assembled group, "We are not letting him drive anywhere. If one of the sober people wants to drive, we'll let you go. If not, we will make sure the police have your license number."

The young man got into the passenger seat, the

woman who had run away returned, one of the young and sober women drove, and Yolanda went back to work.

HOW WE SEE IT

Yolanda displayed one of the many benefits of being well trained in self-defense. You may notice in our success stories that, time and again, there's no fighting involved which runs counter to the classic understanding of physical self-defense. In some of our scenarios, there's not even an immediate threat of harm. It's not hard to predict, however, that drunken driving has *enormous* potential for harm, and Yolanda wasn't about to let a drunk driver not only hurt himself and his passengers but others who use the streets and highways.

As one of our graduates, Yolanda was confident because she knew if the driver were to get violent, she'd be able to handle it. She assessed the situation and saw that she could make a difference... one that would potentially be live-saving.

The risks? Possibly pissing off a young man who was already pissed from alcohol. Could she handle an angry drunk? Yes.

The benefits? Yolanda inadvertently modeled good citizenship that many of us shy away from because of the fear of harm to ourselves. She also showed the three young women they were not helpless, and that — because they were so upset about their male friend — they'd ignored a very simple solution: JUST TAKE THE FRIGGIN' KEYS!

People who are trained in adrenaline-based self-defense programs are able to see simpler and faster solutions because they've been trained to fight under stress. When there's no fight, it's even easier to see solutions in potentially dangerous circumstances.

We'll never know if Yolanda saved lives that night or not. You can't prove what doesn't happen, but you can certainly change the odds of an almost-guaranteed really bad outcome.

Y is for YELLING

Noise is not often considered a self-defense tactic, but indeed it is. While *Yolanda, You're Not Driving,* did not need to yell to assert her authority, the people in need of her assistance did yell to get her attention.

Some of us have alarm systems in our homes. The alarms either set off a loud sound and/or a silent system that alerts a security company when there's been a breach.

By the same token, most of us have our very own handy-dandy alarm systems: our voices! The trick, however, isn't our voice: it's what we *do* with it. We'll admit it: screaming is a bit stereotypical. However, stereotypes be darned, screams can make a big difference if you're intent on making someone leave you alone or to let others know you need help. The problem is, some people ignore screams because they can be mistaken for someone having fun; high pitches are frequently associated with excitement during recreational activities, sports, amusement park rides, parties and the like.

In all of our classes, we teach women, men, girls and boys to *yell* rather than scream. That said, we — **the Safety Godmothers** — admit to having screamed a couple of times despite our best efforts, because it's the sound that came out under stress.

With practice, yelling can become second-nature. We teach the kids in our classes for 6 to 12 year-olds to loudly yell, "No! I — need — help!" as they run away. We work with the women, men and teens in our adult-oriented classes to yell "No!" and to also yell the strikes we teach them as they execute the moves they are learning. It sounds something like this: "No! Groin! Elbow! Eyes!" Sometimes we have them yell the word for the target area; other times, they yell the body part they are using as the target for their strike. Doesn't matter… either one works.

Yelling is good for at least two very important reasons: yelling forces the student, or possible target of violence, to breathe. There's a tendency for all people, when in a stressful situation, to hold their breath. You cannot simultaneously hold your breath and yell at the same time. It's IMPOSSIBLE! Secondly, yelling will get the attention of bystanders and provide the impetus to have other people either help out, or be witnesses for later; the yelling as a "portable alarm system" idea.

We don't know about you, but when we were growing up we were basically told to *never make a scene*. We will allow that throwing a fit in a supermarket isn't right, but we think the ability to "make a scene" is underrated and under-appreciated. Why?

A potential perpetrator of a crime wants two very simple things: to commit the crime and to get away with it, whatever that crime is. The potential victim of a crime has a very potent weapon to make it impossible for the criminal to do that: to make so much noise and to put up such a fuss that they change their mind and go away! Just like the predator going after a nest of baby birds, if it's too much of a hassle, they'll leave.

Are we saying that noise works every time? NO! We never say *anything* works every time. That's fantasyland. However, the more tools you are aware of that are yours to have and to use, the safer you'll be.

Finally, we do know that it's very normal to be concerned about embarrassing yourself. We are pack animals and we want to fit into the pack. Therefore, doing something that draws attention to ourselves is often just mortifying to even think about.

That's why practicing being loud and yelling is so important. We know from many years of experience that practicing being loud, practicing saying things like "No! Back up!" or "No! Go away!" make a difference. That's why we have our students practice verbal skills as much as physical skills. The two go hand in hand in safety practices.

Throughout this book, we've urged you to practice yelling in the mirror. There's a reason we keep bringing it up, so go do it — *right now!* Notice that you might be embarrassed, even if no one else is around. That's our natural reticence. You can grow out of it, but you've got to push through the embarrassment. Practice yelling things like:

- "Back up, sir. You're too close!"
- "No, thank you. Please go away!"
- "You're not listening!"
- "No, I do *not* want to have a drink with you! I'm underage."
- "Go away. If you don't go away, I'll cause a scene!"

Then, practice making a scene!

If you can move through your own embarrassment and do these exercises, there's a much higher possibility you'll be able to deliver if there's an actual incident.

Thankfully, noise is part of our safety toolkit. As it says in the Bible, "Make a joyful noise…" We say, "Make *really* loud safety noises!"

ZACK ZERO TOLERANCE

Zack worked in a pub as both a bartender and part-owner of the popular drinking establishment. Not a large guy, Zack was tough simply from being around the bar scene for years. While he loved the scent of the pub — the smells of ale and smoke — he'd become sick and tired of the frequent macho altercations that would happen when sports-loving, hard-drinking men would get into mischief, especially the kind involving fists. Zack's tolerance for that so-called masculine behavior had reached the zero point, and he was ready to practice peaceful co-existence… or more accurately, resistance to violence.

It was the night after a particularly important soccer match. Zack is English. Patrick was, you guessed it, Irish.

Patrick walks over to Zack, looks him up and down

and says in his finest Irish brogue, "I could beat the crap out of you with one hand tied behind my back. I might just do it, too, because my fellas won."

Zack says, with classic British aplomb, "Indeed you could."

Patrick blusters a bit, looks confused, and then blurts, "Are you making fun of me?" Zack's answer had thrown Patrick. A lot of men would have bristled with the insult, and the fight would have been *on*. But Zack had not followed the "script."

Then Zack takes Patrick's arm and walks him out of earshot from everyone else. "You know," he says conspiratorially, "You really could kick my ass, but we both would probably end up with a black eye, a busted fist, we'd get bloody and feel like crap tomorrow. Why don't you let me buy you a drink and we'll stay friendly."

Patrick agreed and that was that. Zack's zero tolerance for violence worked!

HOW WE SEE IT

You don't always need self-defense training to do the right thing. All you need sometimes is a wee bit of common sense. Zack practiced what we call "target denial." Rather than get caught up in Patrick's antics, he backed down and offered another solution, allowing Patrick the opportunity to save face (and both their faces from bruising!) and removing any antagonism that might have set off the man.

Most male-to-male situations are ego-based. (Heck, a lot of male-to-*female* violence is ego-based.) The typical male altercations or assaults often revolve around things like looking at another man's girlfriend, or a team winning or losing a game, or other "territory" issues. We as a society often expect men to be able to handle themselves, to be able to fight or know how to talk their way out of a bad situation. The problem is, these are skills that must be *learned*, and negotiation skills are not taught at football or baseball practice, other than arguing with the referee or umpire! As a result, subconsciously men feel they must do something… even if the only thing they know how to do is fight.

Zack made a choice based on conscience: he was not going to be a man who indulges in violence, and would find another way to work out the issues that routinely came up in his bar. He did a great job. Zack threw Patrick off his game by not playing by the usual male rules and offering a solution that worked for the aggressor *and* for Zack. It's not rocket science: we call it impulse control. Impulse control is blocked by alcohol, which is why drunks are so unpredictable and volatile; the more you drink, the less impulse control you have. The less impulse control you have, the more likely you are to do stupid things.

We want more men to practice intolerance… intolerance of violence, that is.

Z is for ZERO

One of the most refreshing things about teaching personal safety skills to girls and women, whether verbal or physical, is the opportunity to start at zero with our students. In many endeavors, students have some kind of clue about what they are about to learn, no matter what their age or experience level is. With self-defense, however, we are often able to start with a clean slate — a tabula rasa — which means we don't need to spend a lot of time erasing bad habits and preconceived notions about how to defend oneself. The major experience is one of "Wow! I didn't know *that!*" which is an environment that is fun, empowering and inspiring for everyone involved.

Contrast this innocence with our classes for men and boys, and you see one of the biggest gender gaps our society has: men and boys are culturally *expected* to know about defending themselves *and* their loved ones. Sometimes this is unfair, because non-athletic men and boys often don't know more about defending themselves than women and girls. The athletic males, especially those who play contact sports, have an advantage because they know and have experienced their own physical limits as well as the limits of their teammates. Otherwise, males glean what they can from male relatives, teachers, peers, or from the movies, then often pretend they knew it all along. This creates a lot of gender pressure, and is not a "zero" place to come from when learning anything.

Speaking of movies, if and when we see preconceived notions of fighting from our students, it's almost always because of movies and television and their ubiquitous use of fists. Using fists is a really bad (and *painful*) idea unless you have been specially trained on how to use an ungloved fist. Using fists without gloves is a very quick way to break your hands. There are some very effective uses of fists, but *not* the way you learn from watching movies or TV! To show how pervasive this is, our youngest students — boys *and* girls — already emulate using fists (badly) in our kids' classes. We need to undo that fist habit right away.

We also use "zero" as a metaphor for going from zero to lightning fast in the scenarios that involve an attempted rape. The coaching we give is that, if a perpetrator has us pinned on the bed or ground, we need to breathe, self-talk ourselves into watching for an "opening," and then go from zero to EXPLODE! Imagine someone completely silent, breathing, still as a pond of water, and then... they become 100% sound, fury and dynamic energy. *That's* what we're talking about.

We hear the term "zero tolerance" quite a bit, and as in the story *Zack Zero Tolerance*; it is often used in the arena of personal or public safety. If a school has a zero tolerance policy, for instance, it's often in relationship with zero tolerance of weapons brought to school. Another area of zero tolerance is fighting on the playground. That can be good, but it also has a negative side.

You may recall from grade school that, if a student strikes in self-defense, they may be expelled along with the kid who started it because of a zero tolerance for hitting. In that case, we highly recommend that families have meetings to discuss the family policy toward self-defense, which may differ from the school's. There are hallway and playground bullies that are extremely violent and employ non-childlike forms of bullying, like strangling. These are actually criminal acts: if an adult strangled another adult, they would be arrested for committing a crime.

Later on in life, there is supposedly a zero tolerance climate in the workplace — whether as an intern or an employee — when it comes to sexual or racial harassment. Those who have been the subject or object of humiliation know that harassers are extremely sneaky and good at making their harassment look innocent. While most schools, corporations or workplace environments have a clearly stated policy of "no harassment," **the Safety Godmothers** believe that we as individuals need to practice how to stop harassers *before* it gets to the point where it impacts our studies or work. That is not as easy as it might sound. One of the benefits our students report is they were able to strategize about stopping harassers more effectively after they'd taken our classes.

In some forms of Buddhist practice there is a concept called "The Beginner's Mind," which is another form of zero. The idea is, no matter how much experience you have in something, if you approach it from the mindset of a beginner you will always learn something new ... and stay humble. The mind and body is most receptive to learning when you stop trying to live up to your own or other peoples' expectations... to start from nothing, nada, zip, zed, zilch, zero.

In conclusion, we firmly stand for *our* personal policy of Zero Tolerance, which is: we have Zero Tolerance of disrespect toward, or violence against, *anyone*. We invite you to adopt that policy for yourself.

Ellen's Acknowledgements

I want to take this opportunity to thank *anyone and everyone* who has ever participated in our work. Seriously, I freeze every time I watch an awards show because I share the fear of forgetting people who have been so incredibly helpful to this movie... er, book. That deer in the headlights look? Imagine that on my face as I write this. If, after reading this, it turns out that I have forgotten to mention you, please write your name here:_____. OK, here goes.

I want to thank all the people involved with IMPACT Personal Safety from my first class in 1992 to now, including my very first IMPACT buddy Mary Theresa Migliorelli, who has stayed my buddy to this day. Over the years, scores of women and men have worked as either staff or volunteers (sometimes both) to make our training available to me and thousands of others. This teaching literally saves and heals lives. Thanks also are given to the many people who let us know how they've used our training to make themselves safer in a sometimes unsafe world.

Concerning this book, we want to acknowledge the artistic and graphic genius of Marty Safir, whose aesthetics, skill and design expertise are unsurpassed.

Gavin de Becker was one of the first adopters of my work as

an advocate for, and writer about, personal safety. By writing the foreword to my first book, *Beauty Bites Beast*, he made me "real" in the eyes of readers who wouldn't have otherwise sought me out. And wow! It means a lot to us that he also wrote the foreword for *The Safety Godmothers*. What he generously sent us was so jam packed with wisdom that we decided to divide it into three separate pieces: two alongside our own stand-alone items, and a special "for parents only" segment.

Speaking of Gavin, I'm very grateful to him for my friendship with Robert Martin, whom I would never have met without Gavin. Bob is a great friend, confidante and leader whose leadership will make our work at IMPACT even more available to more people.

I am very proud and grateful regarding my associations with many of the IMPACT chapter heads and leaders in other cities: Kay Dahlstrom Mendick in Grand Forks, North Dakota; Martha Thompson in Chicago; Karen Chasen and Donna Chaitt of PrePare, NYC; Carol Middleton in Washington, DC; Amelia Norfleet Dorn in Denver; Yudit Sidikman of El Halev in Israel; Julie Harmon in Ohio; Lisa Scheff and Ruby Reid of Bay Area IMPACT. These are my dearest sisters who are also on a mission to make personal safety as normal and accessible as water safety classes are now.

I'm thankful that Ger O'Dea uses *Beauty Bites Beast* to help heal his students. I'm grateful to Christopher Roberts for bringing personal safety to so many people all over the English speaking world. He creates a mode of normalcy and a business model for personal safety that is truly inspiring.

It's hard to know where to begin with my thanks to the people I've met through the National Women's Martial

Arts Federation: Anne Kuzminsky, George Schorn, Katy Mattingly, April Miller, Wendi Dragonfire, Cassie Potter Hitzman, Joanne Factor, Kerry Kilburn, Kore Gate, Molly Sacco Hale, Myrna Condon and Zosia Gorbaty. A special shout-out goes to Lee Sinclair, whose international reach is awe-inspiring with both her work in Africa and here in the states.

I'm very proud of our association with Erin Weed, and her outreach to young women on campuses throughout the US with Girls Fight Back. Gina Kirkland has now taken on the GFB mission and I'm tickled to have her as a friend.

I'm very thankful to my entire Landmark Worldwide community, where our dreams are encouraged and empowered. My seminar community is too vast to name individually, but I love my graduate seminars and it's there where I get emotional fuel to keep going. For me, the Landmark Forum has been instrumental in all of my creative endeavors.

Thanks to Deborah Kennedy, the producer of *Beauty Bites Beast: The Documentary*, for her patience as I finished this book.

And then there is my Writers' Workout group of Altadena, CA, where I am the coach, which is another consistent source of inspiration. A big special thanks to Alaine Lowell, Tim Burgess, Gail Libman, Jefferson Black, Ahmed Korayem, Misti Barnes, Carol Woodliff, Paul Elliott and Dianne Williams who sat through many sessions giving invaluable feedback for *The Safety Godmothers*.

While vetting the various versions of this book before it became the one you are currently holding in your hand, we picked readers whom we trusted and who have raised — or who are currently raising — children and adolescents. Thank you so much Paul and Kristi Ronningen for reading the first and oldest draft of this book. Indeed, my North Dakota extended family has been very patient and kind toward my passion in the personal safety realms. Besides Paul and Kristi I thank Signe Snortland, Maren and Josh Stokka, and Marete Snortland-Banks for their special encouragement.

More recent and invaluable readers are Kim Tso, Kristin Maschka, and Kurt Solay who gave us their parental views. Thanks to Annette Helberg for her love, warmth, belief and encouragement.

Georgia Bragg gave us time and insights about *The Safety Godmothers* above and beyond the call of duty. She has been my friend since we were teens. In fact, she was the one who suggested that Lisa and I write a book aimed at young adult readers in the first place. That means she is really the first godmother of this book, for which I am forever grateful. Heartfelt thanks, Georgia.

I always thank Gloria Steinem and Robin Morgan whenever I can. I had the absolute privilege of stumbling upon their activism when I was still in my teens, and their influence turned me into someone who has made my life all about the empowerment of women and kids. I also am grateful to my parents and sisters, *and* Sonja Staley — my 3rd grade teacher — who told me I could be a leader when that wasn't a given for little girls. It's often said that a good teacher can transform a child's life. Sonja did that for me.

This book would not exist without the unbelievable amount of work that Ken Gruberman, a real "Safety Godfather," has done to make this book a reality. He's been a cheerleader, latté maker and most importantly our editor, all along. We really can't thank him enough other than to get this book out to as many people as we possibly can. Also, I have the great fortune to be married to him.

Finally, it's hard writing a book in general, and specifically it's almost impossible to write one with a partner. Giving birth to a book is painstaking, arduous and one must have great patience to take a book on with another person. I can't think of a more *fun*, warm, bold and brilliant writing partner than Lisa Gaeta. What a journey it's been, and I'd embark on another in a heartbeat. (Oh wait, we have!)

Thank you Lisa, for your heart and soul and for the years you've kept IMPACT available for thousands of people. Without your persistence, the world would be a poorer place. You have made a deep, excuse the expression but I just have to say it... *impact* on my life.

Lisa's Acknowledgements

There are so many people to thank for what they contributed to me over the years. As a result, just like Ellen I'm sure I am forgetting someone. If you are someone who knows me well, you know for *certain* I am forgetting something or someone! While I try not to take myself too seriously, I am serious about my gratitude to all of you for being a part of my life and therefore a part of this book. I have learned so many important life-lessons from many of you; a lot of them have been infused into the IMPACT message. So much, in fact, that I could not possibly single out every specific instance. As I'm writing this, I have been teaching IMPACT for almost 30 years: that is a long time, and a lot of people …

First of all, I'd like to thank my biological family — if you've ever had me for a teacher, you've heard stories about some of them. If you are part of my life, you know how important they are to me. Thank you to my mother (whom I miss desperately) and father for their constant, continual and undying love and support over the years. I could not have continued without you; IMPACT, in this form, would not exist if not for you.

To my sister and best friend Rosanne Overton, who has been there for me more times than I can count and in more ways than I can even begin to mention here. To my Aunt Jean, my first role model, who showed me how to be an independent woman *and* that it was OK to be one. To my brother and sister-in-law Paul and Anne Gaeta, and my amazing nieces and nephews who give me hope for future generations: Tony, Brooke, Lauren, Dani, Joe, Jennifer, Patrick, Cory, and Courtney. I don't want to leave out "The Littles": Sofia, Travis and Addy — thank you all!

How do I even begin to thank my chosen family? There are so many of you from so many phases of my life.

Thank you to my current fellow Board of Directors and advisors: Bob Martin, board chair and mentor from whom I've learned so much in such a short time; Christy Adair, John Amussen, Rob Latimer, Donna Wells, and Faye Berriman for all of your time and dedication through some really trying times.

The list of people who have had an influence on IMPACT over the years is long — and I mean *long*. Not only have you supported IMPACT and contributed to the growth and improvement of our program and our system, but you have supported *me* and stuck by me when things got rough. You have been with me and for me in ways most people never get the opportunity to experience. I do not exaggerate when I say I could not have done this without you: Johnny Albano, Roland Arenz, Mike Belzer, Liz Cava, Jeff Chean, Ben Cook, Sylvia Deily, Rondell Dodson, Kat Flesh, Don Hart, Perry Hauck, Heidi Hornbacher, Laura Kaiser, Dennis Lansdon, Randy Mamiaro, Michael Ness, Momi Ono, Michael Penafiel, Clare Randolph, Roxie Rock, Thomas Rodriguez, Francine Russell, Kirk Saiki, Heidi Skvarna, Bobi Thomson (my partner in crime for so many years!), Carla Young, Peter Vance, Ron Vizansky, Greg Weir … just to name a few.

Gavin de Becker has been a great supporter and friend of mine and IMPACT since the early 90s. He has changed the way we look at violence in this country, and there simply aren't enough ways to say "thank you" for that. I have stolen so much material from Gavin over the years, and will continue to do so! Thanks also to *Gavin de Becker & Associates*, who have also been a great group of supporters over the years, especially Ellen Prystajko, Michael LaFever and Jeanette Tran.

To all of my besties — what would I have done without my girlfriends? You have been so supportive and sometimes painfully honest throughout the years. Judy Johnson, Jennifer Bunting and Sascha Ferguson… what can I say that won't get me thrown in jail? I love you more than my luggage! Jeff Grant and Kevin Scott for always being there for me; Craig Ferguson for making me laugh when I wanted to cry; Rana Joy Glickman for your continual support and words of wisdom; Teresa Lichti, Debbie Kane, Addie Mitchell, Andre Miller, Cindy Lemon … can you believe we're all still friends?!

One of the things of which I am most proud is our work with teenagers. We have been able to teach IMPACT to thousands of high school-aged girls and boys because of the following people who believed in our mission and our system of teaching: Julie Napoleon for bringing IMPACT to Marlborough School and making it the first school in the nation to offer self-defense as a full-semester, for-credit PE course; Barbara Wagner for supporting IMPACT at Marlborough all of these years (we are in our 22nd year at Marlborough as I write this); Liz Driscoll for embracing IMPACT and making it part of the PE department at Marymount High School (we are in our 20th year at Marymount as I write this); the amazing team of teachers and supporters of IMPACT at Crossroads: Adam

Behrman, John Climaco, Tom Nolan, David Listenberger, Sheila Bloch, Shawn Gilbert, Margie Macias and Daryl Roper; Kristen Benjamin for bringing IMPACT to Archer School for Girls.

I would be remiss if I didn't thank my ex-husband, Al Potash. You came into my life when I was at an important crossroads, and introduced me to IMPACT which literally changed the course of my life. For that I will be forever grateful.

I am also grateful to Donna Chaiet and Karen Chasen of Prepare in NYC, who kept me in the game when I wanted to leave. IMPACT is alive today because of you. To my colleagues around the country: Julie Harmon in Ohio (my pal forever!); Kaye Mendick in North Dakota; Carol Middleton in Washington DC; Amelia Dorn in Colorado; Ruby Reid and Lisa Scheff from Bay Area, CA; Alena Scheim in New Mexico; Yudit Sidikman of El Halev in Israel; Meg Stone in Massachusetts; Martha Thompson in Illinois — thank you all for your collaboration and dedication. And thank you to Erin Weed, formerly of Girls Fight Back and Gina Kirkland, currently of Girls Fight Back, for spreading the word to so many girls around the country that their lives are worth fighting for, and including IMPACT in your message.

There have been many people over the years from other systems of self-defense and martial arts who have given me invaluable skills that are also infused into the system of IMPACT training: my first-ever sensei and IMPACT Trainer, Danielle Evans; Sensei Cliff Stewart of WAR; Paxton Quigley, my first firearms instructor; Graciela Casillas, my first knife fighting and defense instructor, and the first real-life female badass (!) I ever met; Eric Cobb of Z Health; Arnold Sensei who taught me how to fall; Mark Worland (wait, do you really believe that or are you just saying it to piss me off?) who was a great influence on our weapons class as it is today; Payton Quinn, of RMCAT… thank you all.

I also want to thank Pam and Syd Suggs for their amazing support throughout the years. Thank you for believing in IMPACT!

Thank you to my most influential teachers whose classes gave me the foundation for who I am and what I teach today: Beverly Kelly, who taught me the basics of communication; Edward Tsang, who taught me the art of negotiation and tolerance; and Father Ernest Candalaria who showed me that girls can be leaders.

To my writer's group, thank you so much for tirelessly listening to our stories and topics — sometimes over and over again — and for your straight-forward feedback: Alaine Lowell, Gail Libman, Paul Elliot, Carol Woodliff, Tim Burgess, and Dianne Williams.

Thank you to our readers who gave the first comments on the book as a whole: Christine Piraino, David Brooks (hey cuz!!) and Wade Lichti.

You would not be reading this right now if it weren't for Ken Gruberman, our barista and editor. He put up with a lot of shenanigans from us and never went running and screaming from the room! Also a great thank you to Marty Safir for all of his graphic and artistic work on this project.

And last, but certainly not least, my co-author: Ellen Snortland. How can you thank someone who has been a friend, mentor, teacher and co-author? I'm pretty sure we laugh more than anything else when we are together. Ellen helped me write my first IMPACT Workbook way back in 1992; she taught me that it takes a community to write a simple book. She has been the envoy of the "IMPACT message" for many years, to countless people around the world, and is truly tireless! Ellen changed my life when she explicitly told me "it's okay to love cooking and shopping and wearing high heels and tiaras — all the 'girlie' stuff — *and* also be a total badass who can kick someone's ass!" I am forever grateful for that message and for our friendship!

Gavin de Becker Bio

We are so honored to have Mr. de Becker's contributions to **The Safety Godmothers.** *Accordingly, we thought you should see his full bio, to get a better sense of who he is and what he stands for.*

Gavin de Becker is our nation's best-known expert on the prediction and management of violence. His work has earned him three Presidential appointments and a position on a congressional committee.

He was twice appointed to the President's Advisory Board at the U.S. Department of Justice, and he served two terms on the Governor's Advisory Board at the California Department of Mental Health.

His 375-member consulting firm advises government agencies, universities, police departments, corporations, and media figures on the assessment of threats and hazards. Gavin de Becker & Associates maintains the world's largest library of threat and obsessive communications, consisting of more than 400,000 pieces of material.

Mr. de Becker's first book *The Gift of Fear* was the nation's #1 bestseller, on the New York Times Bestseller List for seventeen weeks. It is now published in thirteen languages. In 2008, Oprah Winfrey dedicated an entire show to commemorating the 10th anniversary of the book's publication.

His second book, *Protecting the Gift: Keeping Children & Teenagers Safe (and Parents Sane)* was the #1 parenting book of 1999.

His post-9/11 book on terrorism, *Fear Less*, was published in 2002 and featured on *Larry King Live*, *The Today Show*, *The O'Reilly Factor*, and *The View*.

Mr. de Becker's most recent book *Just 2 Seconds: Using Time and Space to Defeat Assassins*, presents the result of a study of more than 1400 attacks and incidents involving at-risk people. Though not written for a general public audience, the book has readers in 25 countries.

Mr. de Becker wrote the introduction for *To Have Or To Harm*, the first book on stalking (Warner Books), and for Ellen Snortland's *Beauty Bites Beast: Awakening the Warrior Within Women and Girls*, and he's written more than forty articles and white papers, several of which have been reprinted by the Department of Justice's National Criminal Justice Reference Service.

Mr. de Becker is the designer of the MOSAIC threat assessment systems used to screen threats to Justices of the U.S. Supreme Court, members of Congress, and senior officials of the CIA. Along with the U.S. Marshals Service, he co-designed the MOSAIC system used for assessing threats to Federal Judges and prosecutors. MOSAIC systems are also used by police departments all over America for assessment of spousal abuse cases.

Mr. de Becker has shared his philosophies about prevention of violence in several appearances on the *Oprah Winfrey Show*, *60 Minutes*, *Larry King Live*, and *20/20*. He has also been profiled in *Time* and *Newsweek*, the *Wall Street Journal*, the *New York Times*, and many others.

Mr. de Becker is a Senior Fellow at the UCLA School of Public Affairs, and a Senior Advisor to the Rand Corporation on public safety and justice matters.

Appendix

IMPACT Personal Safety:
What We Do, and Who We Are

People often recognize our fully padded mock assailants and know about our 20 Hour Women's Basics Course, thanks to numerous TV news stories about us; you can see a typical segment at www.impactpersonalsafety.com right there on the main page. We also offer courses to address workplace sexual harassment, leadership training, communication skills, teamwork and bonding, workshops for men, teens and children — all based in training using realistic scenarios.

Our goal is to empower individuals to make effective personal safety choices. In an emotionally supportive environment, students practice both verbal and physical skills with our fully padded mock assailants. With this unique physical training method you can deliver full force, knockout blows to vulnerable areas on the padded assailant's body in dynamic, interactive fights. Training includes verbal self-defense strategies practiced in role-playing scenarios in a variety of contexts: for example, dealing with strangers and with people you know.

Students learn the most common ways individuals are at-tacked, as well as the strategies and psychology of assailants. Classes prepare you mentally and physically to handle the full range of challenging situations we all face in our daily lives, including the danger of extreme circumstances. IMPACT teaches you to avoid danger by heightening your awareness, shorten your body's natural "freeze" response, capitalize on your adrenaline rush, assess situations quickly, respond decisively and so much more.

The benefits of the class go beyond learning how to stay safe or how to intervene in a potentially violent encounter.

Our graduates report positive effects such as greater general awareness and confidence, increased self-esteem and assertiveness, ability to communicate clearly and directly, creative and flexible problem solving skills, more focus and effectiveness at work, and calm, clearheaded thinking during times of stress or crisis.

Our Dream

We dream of providing our training to anyone who wants it. Our training works, and anyone can learn what we teach. We know this because women and girls of all ages, sizes, physical abilities, cultures, races, socio-economic backgrounds, and educational levels have successfully completed our classes. We are daily and painfully aware that not everyone can get access to or afford our education. We are working toward being accessible, affordable and portable!

We are a struggling nonprofit ourselves, and make our bread and butter from currently providing IMPACT education at private schools, because they often have less red tape and more resources than public schools. We want to have our classes available to not only public educational institutions, but shelters for women and children, community centers, public recreational facilities… all the places where people are nurtured and learn in their communities.

We dream of the day when the safety and well-being of women and children has the same priority in our society as sports or entertainment.

How to Choose a Self-Defense Class

We'd like to offer a big "thank you!" to the **National Women's Martial Arts Federation** for their handy guide, *How To Choose a Self-Defense Class*. Go to www.nwmaf.org for more info about this fine organization.

In their original posting of these criteria on the NWMAF website, they thank the National Coalition Against Sexual Assault for some of the following material. **The Safety Godmothers** are aligned with these views, and where we have additional opinions, we will note them.

The NWMAF is a tremendous resource for finding classes all over the world, no matter what gender you are; in the following, when you see "she" and "her", if you are a male you can swap in "he" and "his" when shopping for a class.

* * *

A good self-defense class teaches skills in awareness, assertiveness, verbal confrontation skills, safety strategies, and physical techniques. These strategies can help you prevent, escape, resist and survive assault, abuse or harassment. A good self-defense course provides training in psychological awareness and verbal skills, not just physical strikes.

In choosing a class, look for a program or an instructor who:

- Knows the facts about abuse and assaults aimed at women, and tailors her classes to this reality. For example, a good class will address situations involving acquaintances and romantic partners, not just attacks by strangers.
- Knows the realities of women's lives and is able to work with each student and where they are in their maturity, experience of life, assault history, or physical limitations. For example, a good teacher is able to adapt verbal and physical

techniques to each student's strengths and challenges; she will not have a "one-size-fits-all" program.

- Respects women's decisions on how to handle dangerous or threatening situations and does not blame or judge survivors.
- Offers techniques, knowledge and strategies to help students make their own decisions about how to handle situations. She does not tell students what they should or should not do.
- Takes an empowering approach not only to the practice of self-defense but also to teaching the program. For example, students should be able to determine their own levels of participation in the class, and no one should feel pressured into doing specific exercises.

The Safety Godmothers add this:

We strongly advocate the use of female/male instructor teams, as we believe that ultimately the end of violence against *everyone*, with an initial focus on women and kids, will come about with the partnership of women and men working together.

We certainly acknowledge that a male in a self-defense class setting, especially as the primary instructor, might re-traumatize women who have a fear of men based on their assault history. But time and time again, we have also seen women — while working in our supportive and empowering gender-integrated atmosphere — come to the realization that not all men mean them harm.

We also recognize that there are certain religious affiliations which will not allow for a gender-integrated classroom.

We are grateful there are "female only" self-defense classes available, even though that is not what we generally do. There are IMPACT classes in Israel that have female Padded

Assailants, and there's also an IMPACT chapter in Denver, Colorado that has a female PA.

Speaking of gender, a good thing to notice when selecting a class is if the *only* instructor is a man. These days, it is common to find a hunky guy — often ex-law enforcement or a martial artist — leading self-defense classes for women in gyms, parks and other places. The belief is that women will find the guys attractive and sign up, shelling out some considerable cash in the process.

These men — many of whom have good intentions — typically come from either a military or martial-arts background, and have no clue whatsoever about issues involving women's socialization, their needs, their unique strengths, or even how male-based training techniques "lands" for them. We would only recommend this kind of class as a last resort.

Fortunately, over the last few years a new trend has emerged that veers away from the Hunky Clueless Male Instructor syndrome. We are happy to report there *are* some men who understand the unique needs of women when it comes to self-defense. Specifically, we recommend Ger O'Dea in Edinburgh (www.dynamis-gym.com) and Christopher Roberts of SAFE International in Canada (safeinternational.biz) as providers, because they know that teaching women and girls to prepare for possible violence is vital to a healthy society.

When shopping for a class, use the criteria above to select. Then... go for it!

Important Practices and Conversations

As you know, we want you to take a self-defense class; preferably one of ours. Whether you are able to take a class or not, there are some key practices you need to be aware of, and conversations you need to have with your parents, guardians or those entrusted to your well-being. These practices and conversations form the basis of a **Personal Safety Strategy.**

Exits and Safety

You know how flight attendants ask you to look around and locate the nearest exit when you're on a plane? (It might be behind you!) Or how concert venues ask a similar question before the show starts? We recommend that you notice where exits are, no matter *where* you are: in a mall, park or sports venue. In the same vein, *always* take a moment to memorize where you parked your car, or where your family parked their car.

If you're with friends or family, determine where "safety" is whenever you are out and about; if smaller kids are involved, make sure they know as well. Is it the information kiosk? The clerk at the store? The Disneyland Town Hall? Always agree upon and know where to meet if there is an unintentional separation.

Code Words and Phrases

In 2009, a 17 year old girl was murdered in Los Angeles; the incident breaks our heart every time we think about it. She was kidnapped, and forced to withdraw money at various ATMs. She called each of her parents, both times asking how to use a credit card to withdraw money, only to be told the credit card would not work. Her family had no sense from these calls that she was in trouble. It's possible that if the family had a code word or phrase, she might have gotten away. Please understand that what happened was *not* the family's fault that they didn't have a way to communicate while the teen was in danger. *It's always the criminal's fault.* Nonetheless, it's the best idea to have a conversation with the people you love to plan for the worst.

Come up with a code word or phrase in case a family member or loved one is in danger or outside their safety zone. Come up with something that's easy to remember and that can be said on the phone, in front of the unsafe person. For example, if you say, "Is Molly home?" and you know that you don't have a Molly in your family, and you've agreed that "Is Molly home?" equals *I need help, come get me,* you know you need to take action. This is equivalent to pulling a family safety "fire alarm," and must be used only in emergencies. Remember that the word or phrase must make sense *in context*: agreeing to say "banana" would alert the unsafe person that there's a code being used. Only entrust this code to trustworthy people.

Zero Tolerance policies in schools and at work places

Please discuss with your family what the family approach is to physical self-defense. Almost all schools and workplaces have a zero tolerance policy, and there are consequences for using force — even if the force is used strictly for self-defense. If you or a child in your family is experiencing a level of harassment that includes force, are your parents or guardians willing to back you or them, and face the consequences if a shin kick, blow to the solar plexus or foot stomp is the best way to stop the harassing behavior? This is an important discussion to have during all phases of life, starting at about age 5.

Origins of IMPACT Personal Safety

We at IMPACT Personal Safety are definitely *not* anti-martial arts; our originators were all martial artists, and we are grateful for the contributions that many traditionally trained martial artists have made to all of us. That said, most martial arts "models" didn't include elements we now think are essential to women's self-defense, like factoring in the issues of gender and socialization. Rigid rules and notions of correct martial arts "form" tend to be more suited to sports and athletics than the realities of actual attacks.

The origins of most martial arts, from all over the world, are fascinating and not what most think: the lower classes of people were denied access to traditional weapons of warfare and were oppressed by the leading or ruling class. So these oppressed groups trained themselves to use the tools of everyday life — for example, *nunchaku*, or nunchucks as they are commonly called, were a threshing tool used to harvest grain — and practiced various fighting skills while working in the fields, etc., to form a resistance and fight their way out of oppression. And yes, they were developed by men for men in — you guessed it — male-to-male combat.

Our originators created the foundation upon which IMPACT Personal Safety and its researchers built this particular type of self-defense training. The team of researchers we refer to encompasses a group of Psychologists, Martial Artists, Sociologists, Engineers and Educators, as well as others, who all have continuous input into the evolution of our training.

The Safety Godmothers do not purport to speak for all of the IMPACT chapters around the country, nor express all the views contained within this book. This is especially true of our "origins," since there are differing opinions within any dynamic and evolving movement such as ours.

When we branched off and became "IMPACT Personal Safety," we chose a name that would exemplify our work and describe our courses — a name that would stand out. IMPACT is less about how we impact the assailant with our strikes and more about how the program IMPACTS our lives. It gives one a sense of power, strength and freedom; not only does the information IMPACT our personal safety, but it will IMPACT the rest of our lives. And that means *all* aspects of our lives, including both personal and professional.

There are four fundamental points that were influential in the development of the IMPACT courses that addressed why traditional martial arts often do not meet the needs of women when they are attacked, and why women needed their own form of self-defense. They are still as relevant today as when we started, which is why our training is always evolving:

Attack Strategy — One of the greatest fears women have is being attacked from behind by an assailant who then drags her into the bushes. While we know this is not the most common way women are attacked, we address this scenario first for various reasons; mostly because, if you can conquer your greatest fear on the first day of class, imagine what you can do for the rest of the 20 hours! We address the "real" ways that women are attacked; we use scenarios and role-playing that allows the student to feel what it's like to really fight for her life. For example, the most common stranger situation is what we call "the interview" or the "confrontation" where the assailant tries to have a conversation with the potential victim to see if she is a good choice for an assault. We learn to talk and, if necessary, fight our way out of these situations. We also deal with the far more common situation where the student is acquainted with their attacker, which has a completely different dynamic.

Physiology — Women's bodies are built differently than men's. Shocking, we know, but there it is. Physiologically speaking, women tend to be stronger in their lower bodies, their hips and legs, than in their upper bodies. So it makes sense that we would teach women to use the strongest areas of their bodies.

Realism — We believe that full force training, training to fight the way you would in a real-life situation, is necessary for a realistic defense. (Many women have not even had the benefit of contact sports to give them some kind of experience of what it feels like to hit, or be hit, on a field or court.) The way you train is apt to be the way you will respond in a real confrontation.

Socialization — Women have been socialized to not hurt another person, even if that person is hurting them. We have been told that "ladies don't fight," "don't hit your brother there," and more. We have been told that we are helpless, that women cannot defend themselves. We have even been told that we should not fight back, we should be passive and try not to anger the rapist or attacker. By the way, men are not given that advice; they are always expected to defend themselves.

Because women have been so pervasively socialized in this manner, we found this was often the hardest area to address. We realized that we had to somehow incorporate into the course a way to teach women that they have the right to fight for their safety. YOU have the right to defend yourself, and YOU are worth fighting for!

We are proud to say that our origins were truly a community effort, and we are thrilled that, by reading this book, you are now joining this community!

Ellen's Columns on Self Defense

This list contains the column title, the beginning sentence or paragraph of the column, the section it appears in, the date of publication and finally the URL as of this book's publication. Dates are in year.month.day format:

The Danger Of Anti-Rape Wear — Susan B. Anthony, the mother of the women's vote in the U.S. said: "I declare to you that woman must not depend upon the protection of man, but must be taught to protect herself, and there I take my stand." Ms. Anthony said that more than one hundred years ago. She did not say: "Don your chastity belts, girls!" — Politics | 2013.11.26
www.huffingtonpost.com/ellen-snortland/got-medieval-weve-got-a-b_b_4306007.html

I'm Sorry... Not! — One of my New Year's resolutions is to stop saying a "sorry" that's empty... — Impact | 2012.01.27
www.huffingtonpost.com/ellen-snortland/not-saying-sorry_b_1220605.html

No Excuses — We all have excuses for why we haven't accomplished this or that. This is the case with many aspects of the most important revolution on the planet: the end of gender domination. — Impact | 2010.11.30
www.huffingtonpost.com/ellen-snortland/no-excuses_b_790124.html

Learn To Say 'No' — "A man of quality is not threatened by a woman for equality." That's a familiar bumper sticker slogan for some of us. Men are crucial to any social movement, especially the gender equality revolution.

That's kind of a no-brainer, right? — Impact | 2010.08.09
www.huffingtonpost.com/ellen-snortland/learn-to-say-
no_b_676362.html

One Too Many — The murder of Chelsea King drives
home the need to teach kids how to defend themselves. By
making personal safety courses standard nationwide, many
assaults could be prevented. — Impact | 2010.03.18
www.huffingtonpost.com/ellen-snortland/one-too-
many_b_504853.html

Sexual Assault Prevention Tips Guaranteed to Work —
This piece is an answer to the complaint "Why do I have
to learn how to defend myself? Men should stop attacking
women." — Impact | 2010.03.01
www.huffingtonpost.com/ellen-snortland/send-this-to-
everyone-you_b_479481.html

Vaccine For Violence — I dream that learning the
basics of physical self-defense will be a part of everyone's
personal and public policy health care agenda. — Impact
| 2010.01.21
www.huffingtonpost.com/ellen-snortland/vaccine-for-
violence_b_432046.html

Celebrating International Human Rights Day by
saying "No" — Those who reject violence within their
own families are human rights activists... — World |
2009.12.10
www.huffingtonpost.com/ellen-snortland/celebrating-
international_b_387937.html

Roman Polanski, Have I Got a Sentence for You! —
Why don't you help me and my colleagues in the personal

safety community get the word out about a person's human right to protect themselves... — Entertainment | 2009.10.16
www.huffingtonpost.com/ellen-snortland/roman-polanski-have-i-got_b_324050.html

Adjusting Insurance Company Attitudes — For battered women in some states... — Politics | 2009.10.06
www.huffingtonpost.com/ellen-snortland/adjusting-insurance-compa_b_310538.html

Boys Bite Beast — Women and girls need men and boys who are willing to articulate the injustice they see toward their mothers, sisters... — Healthy Living | 2009.08.21
www.huffingtonpost.com/ellen-snortland/boys-bite-beast_b_264682.html

License to Live: Time to make Self-Defense Training a Required Part of Getting a Driver's License — We need the basics of knowledge about violence before we get a license to drive. — Healthy Living | 2009.08.06
www.huffingtonpost.com/ellen-snortland/license-to-live-time-to-m_b_253316.html

Rites of Spring (Ellen Snortland & Gavin de Becker) — Springtime has its rituals, including affluent parents touring college campuses with their daughters and sons to "shop" for the best college or university. Mom and Dad scope out the campus their progeny will call home for the next 4 years. They visit the dorms or off-campus housing. And since all parents want their children to be safe, they might even ask about campus security even though they are entrusting their defensively illiterate kids into an environment that can't realistically keep them safe at all times or under all circumstances. — Healthy Living | 2009.06.02 **www.huffingtonpost.com/ellen-snortland-and-gavin-de-becker/rites-of-spring_b_210154.html**

References Worth Researching

The Safety Godmothers know that the "References" section of a book is usually the least interesting part, and can be off-putting, boring or extremely dry. That is *not* how we roll!

We put this section in for a couple of reasons. (1): there are some very important subjects we've highlighted in this book that deserve more in-depth coverage, and (2), we've made some bold assertions throughout the book and want our readers (and anyone else who is interested) to know the facts behind them. Hence, these pages. We invite you to use the information here as a springboard for your own Knowledge Expansion Project in the areas of women's self-defense, personal safety, human rights and more.

• THE UN's UNIVERSAL DECLARATION OF HUMAN RIGHTS

The United Nations' *30 Articles of the Universal Declaration Of Human Rights* is an international agreement, and not a law. They were proclaimed and adopted by all the governments of the world in 1948, and re-affirmed by them in 1993. Article 3 says "Everyone has the right to life, liberty and security of person." Your right to be safe has been declared a Basic Human Right by all the governments of the world... how cool is *that*? Of course, not everyone got this memo, which is why there are programs like IMPACT Personal Safety. The point is, learning to defend yourself both verbally and physically isn't just a good idea: it's your *right* to do so. Puts a different spin on it, don't you think?

To see all the Articles, learn the history of how the UDHR came to be and more, go to www.un.org/en/documents/udhr/index.shtml

• DOES TEACHING GIRLS SELF-DEFENSE REALLY WORK? YES! AND NOW WE HAVE THE PROOF

The Safety Godmothers have known for decades how effective self-defense is for girls, women, kids and yes, men too. We've seen the proof in every class we've given: people walk in one way, and walk out another. They are literally transformed by the training. And from time to time our students send us success stories, many of which have appeared in this book.

However, all these experiences are anecdotal. Unfortunately, we've never been able to mount a study that could follow our graduates for many years to see what happens in their lives. If we had such a study, it would be the "smoking gun" as it were, finally statistically proving how effective self-defense training is for girls and *disproving* the naysayers. Guess what? We now have such a study! And it came from an unlikely source: Africa.

We consider this *incredibly* important news, and therefore we've chosen to include the entire Reuters news story right here, right in front of your eyes. Here's the link to the story … tinyurl.com/Kenya-Study

One other interesting thing about this article: in it, a prominent doctor states that self-defense is like a "vaccine" against violence. Safety Godmother Ellen Snortland wrote extensively about that very topic … twenty years ago! You'll find it in chapter 17 of her book "Beauty Bites Beast: Awakening The Warrior Within Women And Girls." A brand-new 3rd edition of the book, considered a classic in its field, will soon be available in both physical and Kindle versions on Amazon.com.

Rape-prevention program cuts sexual assaults in Kenya

(Reuters Health) — Self-defense and empowerment classes designed to arm girls with tools to prevent rape reduced sexual assaults among Kenyan students, a new study shows.

The number of rapes dropped 38 percent among adolescents living in high-crime Nairobi settlements 10 months after the classes began, the study found.

In addition, half of the nearly 2,000 girls enrolled in the intervention classes reported using skills learned in the program to stop a total of 817 sexual assaults, according to results published in Pediatrics.

"This is the first time anyone's proven you can prevent rape with a simple, low-cost intervention," Dr. Jake Sinclair told Reuters Health. "It's like a vaccine."

Sinclair, a pediatrician at John Muir Medical Center in Walnut Creek, California, and his wife, Lee Paiva, of *No Means No Worldwide*, created the series of classes after witnessing what they described as an epidemic of rape in Kenya.

Two sexual-assault researchers who were not involved with the current study said it highlights the potential and cost-effectiveness of self-defense classes for vulnerable students all over the world.

"I think this kind of training should be available to all girls and women," sociologist Jocelyn Hollander, from the University of Oregon in Eugene, told Reuters Health. "This is a way to reduce the rate of sexual assault on campus. It really needs to be not just in college but in high school and middle school."

Stanford University School of Medicine researchers in California designed, implemented and oversaw the data collection in the

Kenyan study.

"When we looked at the data, we were very startled and pleasantly surprised. It's amazing," Dr. Yvonne Maldonado told Reuters Health. Maldonado is the senior author of the study and a Stanford pediatrics professor.

She said she envisions the program being used in a variety of settings — from schools and college campuses to the military.

A White House report issued in January estimates that nearly one in five American women — about 22 million — have been raped in their lifetimes. The attacks are particularly prevalent on college campuses, where one in five female students is sexually assaulted, the report says.

Programs like the one in the Kenyan study "should be made more readily available for women until sexual assault victimization rates are substantially reduced," Leanne Brecklin, who studies rape prevention at the University of Illinois Springfield, told Reuters Health in an email.

"Unfortunately, even though there are a lot of courses offered across the U.S., self-defense programs are still not readily available to girls and women across the country or even on most college campuses," she said.

In Kenya, the researchers enrolled 1,978 female students between the ages of 13 and 20 in 12 hours of empowerment training over six weeks. The students also received two-hour refresher courses three, six and 10 months later.

A comparison group of 428 adolescents took a 90-minute life-skills class. Currently the national standard in Kenya, the class touches on a range of topics, from sexual assault to sanitation and food safety.

Almost 18 percent of the girls who took the rape-prevention classes and 14 percent of girls in the comparison group reported being raped in the year before the program began.

That rate fell to 11 percent among girls who received the training almost a year after the program, but remained the same in the comparison group.

The authors calculate that the program cost $1.75 for each rape prevented and compare that to the $86 cost for one post-rape visit to a Nairobi hospital. The $86 does not include the cost of rape-related pregnancies and sexually transmitted infections, including HIV, nor does it take into account the psychological consequences for women who are assaulted.

"It costs us $1.75 to stop a rape," Sinclair said in a telephone interview from Kenya. "That's on the cost-effectiveness level of the smallpox vaccine."

Even girls who were sexually assaulted following the intervention showed signs of benefiting from the program. They were more likely to disclose assaults, enabling them to get support and medical care and possibly leading to identification and prosecution of the perpetrators, the researchers say.

The disclosure rate in the intervention group rose from 56 percent before the classes to 75 percent after them.

Prior research in the U.S. indicates that women and children trained in empowerment and self-defense are more likely to report having confidence and control over their lives and less likely to experience sexual assault, the authors of the current study write.

A pilot study of the current program showed participants were less than half as likely to be assaulted afterward.

The program, developed by *No Means No Worldwide*, includes role-playing, facilitated discussions and training in setting boundaries and developing assertiveness, physical defenses and verbal skills.

"There's a huge arsenal girls can employ that starts with awareness. Girls have the power within themselves to prevent rape. You just have to give them the permission and the skills," Sinclair said.

He said the program also teaches girls to avoid risky situations like walking down a dark street while talking on a cellphone.

"We just believe in girl power," program designer Paiva told Reuters Health.

"If we teach girls, they'll do the rest," she said. "There's so much more going on in these classes that's not about kicking and punches. It's about standing up for yourself, knowing what to say, knowing your rights, speaking up for yourself."

SOURCE: bit.ly/1qYM9Vh Pediatrics, online April 14, 2014.

• "NOT ALONE": PRESIDENT OBAMA'S PROGRAM FOR STAYING SAFE AT SCHOOL

After decades of government inaction regarding campus assaults and rapes, 2014 saw a *radical* shift when the Obama White House created a special task force and a program to go with it: NotAlone. They even created a special public service announcement featuring dozens of celebrities, called "1 Is 2 Many." Here's more info on what they did, and how they are addressing the situation:

"NotAlone was launched in connection with the White House Task Force to Protect Students from Sexual Assault. The Task Force was established on January 22, 2014 — and since then, thousands of people have shared their stories and ideas about how best to eliminate sexual assault on our campuses and schools.

The website contains information for students, schools, and anyone interested in finding resources on how to respond to and prevent sexual assault on college and university campuses and in our schools. Go there to explore, see the public service announcement, find a crisis service, learn more about your rights and how to file a complaint, and view a map of resolved school-level enforcement activities."

www.notalone.gov

• THE CLERY ACT, COLLEGES, UNIVERSITIES, AND YOU

Are you going off to college, or are "college shopping" with your family, and wondering which ones are safe? Until recently it was almost impossible to find out which college campuses were doing anything about campus rapes and assaults ... but now, thanks to The Clery Act, they *have* to tell you.

Here's an edited version of what the Wikipedia says about it:

"The Jeanne Clery Disclosure of Campus Security Policy and Campus Crime Statistics Act or Clery Act is a federal statute that requires all colleges and universities that participate in federal financial aid programs to keep and disclose information about crime on and near their respective campuses. Compliance is monitored by the United States Department of Education, which can impose civil penalties, up to $35,000 per violation, against institutions for each infraction and can suspend institutions from participating in federal student financial aid programs.

"The law is named for Jeanne Clery, a 19-year-old Lehigh University freshman who was raped and murdered in her campus residence hall in 1986. The backlash against unreported crimes on numerous campuses across the country led to the Clery Act, which was signed into law in 1990."

Here is a link to the Clery Center for Campus Security — clerycenter.org — click on the Policy tab to see a summary of the law.

And here's a bonus: would you like to which colleges and universities are accused of mishandling sexual assault cases? You can see a handy InfoGraphic here:

tinyurl.com/ml5zsug

Not surprisingly, the majority of the schools in question are on the east coast in general, and specifically in the Ivy League. Looks like the term "Ivy League Education" has now taken on a new meaning, and not a good one.

• WHAT ARE THE LAWS REGARDING SELF-DEFENSE?

From a legal standpoint, what can and can't you do when it comes to protecting yourself? When do you cross the line from "defense" to offense"? There isn't enough room in this book to list the laws for all 50 states; however, as we live in California, and California laws are similar to many other states, we are listing them here for your perusal.

Section 197 of the California Penal Code lays out the requirements for self-defense. Because self-defense is invoked in the killing of another person, it is listed in chapter one of the penal code which deals with homicide. California's self-defense statute is comparatively lengthy, with the addition of sections 198 and 198.5 which further clarify the preceding four parts of section 197. California also includes as part of section 197 a provision on the use of deadly force during a riot. Section 198.5 provides what is known by legal scholars as a "Castle Doctrine" which modifies the standards for self-defense when it occurs in a home.

According to California law, you act in lawful self-defense if you:

1. Reasonably believe that you are in imminent danger of being killed, seriously injured, or unlawfully touched,
2. Believe that immediate force is necessary to prevent that danger, and
3. Use no more force than necessary to defend against that danger.

California self-defense law justifies your injuring (or even killing) another person if these conditions are satisfied. This means that if these requirements are met, self-defense can serve as a complete defense to a California violent crime if you are forced to kill or injure another.

It should be noted that California self-defense law not only protects you against attacks from people, but also from animals. If you defend yourself against imminent danger coming from a dog attack, for example, any reasonable measures you take to protect yourself will be excused.

• WHY DOES GETTING KICKED IN THE GROIN HURT MEN SO MUCH?

IF you're a man reading this, you already know the incredible pain associated with getting hit in the nads. If you're a girl or woman who grew up with brothers, you probably also don't need much convincing. We've found over the years that the only people who are doubtful about the efficacy of a good swift knee to the groin of a male attacker are those who did not grow up with male siblings. They often ask us if these techniques really work. If there are men present when that question is asked, the answer is always immediate and unanimous: "oh *hell* yes!"

That said, does anyone really know *why* it hurts so much? Up until recently, that answer was shrouded in mystery. Now that we are in the 21st Century, science has finally answered this age-old question. Check out the following link and be prepared for an incredible journey, along with at least a dozen euphemisms for male testes. You've gotta love science!

tinyurl.com/science-explains

• THE NATIONAL CRIME VICTIMIZATION SURVEY

Since 1973, the US Justice Department has been regularly surveying the American public and US law enforcement officials to compile accurate statistics on domestic violence, sexual assaults and violent crime in general, especially as it relates to women. The incredibly unwieldy title for this study is the NCVS: the National Crime Victimization Survey; the latest update happened in 2012. You can find it here — www. bjs.gov/index.cfm?ty=dcdetail&iid=245 — but be prepared to wade into some very deep water.

Fortunately, there are others who have done much of the "heavy lifting" for us by sifting through the immense amount of data generated by this study over the decades. There is a great summary of the study's findings that either passively or actively resisting an assault is an effective strategy, especially for women, which you can read by going to :

www.holysmoke.org/sdhok/rape017.htm

• THE HIGH PROBABILITY OF SURVIVING GUNSHOT WOUNDS

Here is the New York Times article that cites both anecdotal and hard evidence gathered from a variety of ER and trauma doctors, along with specialists, about people who were shot and survived — which was most of them. Why? Check this out and see for yourself:

tinyurl.com/NYT-gunshot

• THE EUROPEAN UNION'S ASTOUNDING STUDY ON DOMESTIC VIOLENCE

In 2010, the European Union issued a ground-breaking report on domestic violence: how prevalent it is and what public attitudes are regarding "DV" as it's also called. We've included the Executive Summary, and if you find it interesting you can read the entire report, which is both fascinating and unnerving: tinyurl.com/EU-DV-2010

Executive Summary

The aim of this survey is to measure the evolution of European public opinion concerning domestic violence against women since 1999, which can be seen as the starting point for collecting information about the public s view on this important problem. Evolutions are particularly interesting to study considering the changing legal context over the past ten years. The first important message that comes out of the study is the rising awareness of Europeans. The survey also shows broad support for EU action in this area.

- 98% of people are now aware of domestic violence across the EU compared to 94% in the previous survey.
- Awareness of domestic violence against women is very

high across the EU, thanks to media such as television (92%), newspapers and magazines (59%) informing the vast majority of EU citizens about the problem.

- Domestic violence remains very common: one respondent in four across the EU knows a woman among friends or in the family circle who is a victim of domestic violence. Since the previous survey, the proportion of Europeans (on a comparable EU15 basis) that say they know a victim of domestic violence in their circle of friends or family has increased from 19% to 25%.

- One person in five knows of someone who commits domestic violence in their circle of friends and family (21%).

- Women are more likely than men to know a woman who has suffered from domestic violence. They are also more likely than men to be aware of people who commit this crime, and more likely to view the problem seriously and to advocate tougher penalties for those responsible.

- 78% of Europeans recognize that domestic violence is a common problem.

- Attitudes to domestic violence have generally become much tougher, with far more people (86%, up from 63% for the EU15) now saying that domestic violence is unacceptable and should always be punishable by law. In the European Union as a whole, 84% consider that domestic violence is unacceptable and should always be punishable by law.

- Sexual and physical violence are seen as the most serious forms of violence suffered by women with 85% of respondents in both cases considering that these are very serious .

- There is strong support for EU involvement in eradicating domestic violence against women (87% of respondents feel that the EU should probably or definitely be involved).

- However, while most people believe that laws are in place

to prevent domestic violence, very few (14%) are familiar with specific EU measures to tackle the problem.

• WHEN IT COMES TO LISTENING TO YOUR "GUT FEELINGS," WE TOLD YOU SO

All through this book, we have told you about how Mother Nature gave you what Gavin de Becker calls "The Gift of Fear" to keep you safe in threatening situations. It can be called "instinct," a "gut feeling," or just the feeling that something is wrong, and is often accompanied by physical sensations such as the hair on the back of your neck standing up, goose bumps and the like.

You cannot manufacture these sensations or will them to happen: they only happen when you're in either perceived or real danger. That's why we constantly remind people to listen to what their bodies are saying, and respect the voice that says "this doesn't feel right."

To end our Reference Section, here's an edited version of a recent news story from CNN that proves these axioms quite convincingly. You can read the entire article here: <u>tinyurl.com/CNN-gut-instinct</u>

Police: Woman's gut feeling thwarts planned school massacre, family murder

by Ben Brumfield / CNN

(CNN) — When Chelsie Shellhas saw a tall young man slip into a storage locker and shut the door behind him one evening this week, it just looked wrong. She dialed 911.

Her instincts were right: Behind the door were bomb-making materials, police in Wacesa, Minnesota, said Thursday. Her call thwarted a cunningly planned gun and bomb attack at a school.

John David LaDue, 17, was looking to carry it out in the coming weeks, police said in an official statement.

After Shellhas' call on Tuesday, officers arrived at the storage park to find LaDue among an assortment of gunpowder, pyrotechnic chemicals, ball bearings and a pressure cooker, police said.

CNN does not usually publish the names of minors charged with crimes but is naming LaDue in this case, because his name has been widely reported in his community.

First, LaDue was planning to kill his father, mother and sister. He had also planned to set off "numerous bombs" during the lunch hour at Waseca Junior/Senior High School, then kill the school resource officer, police said. Then he'd unleash gunfire on students until police officers arrived, allegedly planning to let them kill him.

Shellhas and others in her building first saw the young man in their backyard, Shellhas' cousin Katy Harty told CNN's Brooke Baldwin. "It's scary; we're both, like, really glad that we did call and didn't just shrug it off," she said.

IMPACT Student Statements, Quotes and Survey Responses

Over the years we've collected hundreds, if not thousands, of student testimonials. Some are statements that our students provided for our newsletter or website, and some are answers to our survey that IMPACT students are given at graduation. We've collected some of our favorites here: you may see yourself in some of them.

STATEMENTS

I TOOK TAE KWON DO *for eleven years and was a black belt by age thirteen. I'd broken boards and bricks and fought in tournaments and knew hundreds of techniques. I thought I was a total badass. But my first day of class with IMPACT I realized that, if mugged on the street, breaking a wooden board and doing a spinning-heel kick weren't really going to help me much. What I learned in Tae Kwon Do was how to defend an ancient art, and that's cool. But what I learned in IMPACT was how to defend my life, and that is badass. — Sophie S.*

BEFORE THE IMPACT CLASS, *I didn't know much about self-defense. The only thing I knew was about was the concept of "fight or flight," but I didn't actually know how to fight. — Linzey P.*

WHEN I TOLD A *cousin that I had my tween and teen daughters take a self-defense class, he said "Why would you traumatize them like that"? After I showed him the video recording of their fights, he retracted the statement. He could clearly see they weren't traumatized! What convinced him was the way Nancy, my oldest daughter,* dramatically flipped her ponytail after head-butting her rear-grab assailant. — Shelly C.

DURING MY FIRST SEMESTER of college, a few months after graduating from IMPACT, my friend and I were walking back from the library to our dorm room around 10pm. On our way home, a man whistled at us. We ignored it, thinking it was no big deal, and continued on our way. A minute later, the same man, who I had kept my eye on, approached us. He asked us if we wanted to come with him to a party. My friend shied away and tried to ignore him. When he asked again, I calmly, but boldly, said, "no thank you," and we continued walking back to my dorm room. The man moved in front of us, intentionally blocking our path. He said, "You guys really need to come with me to this party." At this point, my gut and intuition were screaming at me. Without any thought, my hands automatically raised and I was in ready stance. Then I forcefully said, "No. We are not interested. Please move." He stood there for a second, seemingly confused by my hands and booming voice, and then blustered, "OK bitch, you're fat anyway," and walked away in the opposite direction. I couldn't help thinking that he was nothing but a coward. — Taylor P.

QUOTES

THE MOST VALUABLE LESSON for me was learning to believe in myself and trust my instincts.

I HAVE TAKEN SEVERAL martial arts classes in the past and always felt like something was missing. They were so structured and choreographed. Very unrealistic. This class teaches you how to defend yourself in real-world situations.

EVERY MOTHER SHOULD TAKE *this class with her daughter. It is the greatest gift you can give to them.*

I WANT TO TELL *all my friends to take this class and be safe! I feel stronger and safer. Less shy.*

I'VE FELT AN INCREDIBLE *transformation in my confidence and my awareness.*

I FEEL SAFE AND *ready to deal with whatever confrontations come my way.*

I TOOK THIS CLASS *because I knew that I'd be one of those victims who would freeze up, especially in a rape situation. Now that's not me.*

MY BIGGEST BREAKTHROUGH WAS *learning that I was able to defend myself despite being smaller than most.*

I LEARNED THAT MY *life is worth fighting for! I am already recognizing when I am uncomfortable and honoring that.*

THE MOST VALUABLE LESSON *for me was to always keep fighting.*

I WILL BE MUCH *better at setting boundaries with people who are testing and pushing them.*

SURVEY RESPONSES

What did you expect to get out of taking the class?

- Katherine L. — *I expected to be a more confident young woman who will not tolerate any harassment.*

- Natalia P. — *I expected to learn how to defend myself, but I also healed and am now able to have healthier relationships.*

- Claire T. — *I expected to know how to defend myself at any time. I am not even halfway through the course and I have learned so much more!*

- Janan P. — *I expected IMPACT to be a little less intense, but I'm glad it isn't.*

What has been the scariest part of taking the class?

- Erin O. — *The scariest part of taking this class is realizing that people suffer every day from rape and not being able to defend themselves.*

- Natalia P. — *The scariest part was the first day we fought. Standing there waiting to be grabbed… but the second he grabbed me, I fought back and realized how strong I was.*

- Claire T. — *The scariest moment was when I fought for the first time, but after I conquered my fear I actually never really felt like that again… I was actually very excited.*

What advice would you give someone who was thinking about taking the class?

- Katherine L. — I advise them to turn their fear into excitement and get ready for action!

- Natalia P. — I would tell them to take it! Every girl should be shown how strong they are.

- Aly I. — Don't be afraid. It's a learning process.

- Claire T. — I would say take it because it changes your life and how you see things in a good way. And even if you think you don't want to know, or don't care, after you take just one class I believe you will change your perspective.

- Janan P. — DO IT! You'll thank me later.

What has been the most fun for you in taking the class?

- Ava A. — The most fun part of this class has been realizing that I can protect myself if someone wants to hurt me.

What are the 3 most important things you have learned from class?

- Amy M.
  1. Fear is good
  2. Trust your instincts
  3. Think when you are in a dangerous situation

- Janan P.
  1. How to fight
  2. How to talk my way out of bad situations
  3. That it is OK to be afraid.

- Anonymous
  1. Using my voice to yell and make noise while fighting
  2. Using verbal skills to dissuade possible attackers.
  3. Knowing that I am definitely powerful and strong enough to defend myself.

What has surprised you the most about the class?

- Frankie M. — How strong I am! I always thought I was so weak.

- Natalia P. — How supportive the girls are!

- Kat T. — I have more power than I thought I had.

- Anonymous — I have been surprised by the power behind my kicks and all my physical self-defense. I was also pleasantly surprised by the positive energy, supportive atmosphere and camaraderie that our class has developed together.

Do you recommend this class? If so, why?

- Amy M. — Yes. You not only learn important strategies for dangerous situations but you learn about yourself: your boundaries, strength and confidence.

- Natalia P. — Yes! Every girl needs to be educated about this and know how to defend themselves and realize how strong they are.

What has been the hardest part of the class for you?

- Janan P. — The verbal, because I don't like being yelled at. And if you yell at me, I'll yell right back. But apparently, that is incorrect.

What is your favorite skill from class?

- Amy M. — By learning all of the skills, I have been able to be more confident in myself… therefore, they are **all** my favorites!

Safety Godmothers Survey for Readers of this Book

Now that you've read this book, as promised we will leave you with something to think about for your own journey through life. This survey is based on the same one we give our students after graduating from our various classes.

Before reading *The Safety Godmothers*, what did you already know about self-defense?

_____

_____

_____

Why did you read *The Safety Godmothers*?

_____

_____

What did you expect to get out of reading this book?

_____

_____

_____

Was there anything that scared you when reading *The Safety Godmothers*?

_____

_____

What advice would you give someone who was thinking about reading this book?

_____

_____

What has been the most fun for you in reading *The Safety Godmothers?*

_____

_____

What are the 3 most important things you have learned from this book?

_____

_____

_____

What has surprised you the most about *The Safety Godmothers?*

_____

_____

_____

Do you recommend this book? If so, why?

_____

_____

_____

What has been the hardest part of reading *The Safety Godmothers* for you?

_____

_____

What is your favorite skill from this book?

_____

_____

We Want to Hear from You!

Now that you've read our book, you have also joined a special community of people committed to the empowerment and safety of women and girls around the world. We want you to add your voice to the global conversation.

If you've got a question, just ask it. If you have something to say, we want to hear it. If you have a success story that's based on something you read here, or as the result of having taken self-defense training, we *really* want to hear it!

Your Safety Godmothers are just a click away:

OUR WEBSITE

www.thesafetygodmothers.com

OUR EMAIL ADDRESSES

ellen@thesafetygodmothers.com

lisa@thesafetygodmothers.com

OUR TWITTER ACCOUNT

@safetygodmother

OUR FACEBOOK PAGE

www.facebook.com/safetygodmothers

IMPACT PERSONAL SAFETY'S WEBSITE

www.impactpersonalsafety.com

Made in the USA
San Bernardino, CA
16 July 2014